THE POEMS OF
ROBERT BURNS

THE POEMS OF
ROBERT BURNS

*Selected and with an Introduction
by DeLancey Ferguson*

*Decorated with Wood Engravings
by Joan Hassall*

NEW YORK:
THE HERITAGE PRESS

ROBERT BURNS
AND SCOTTISH LITERATURE

ROBERT BURNS was the eldest child of William Burnes* (1721–
1784), a gardener and tenant farmer, and his wife, Agnes Broun
Burnes (1732–1820). Both were of sturdy peasant stock; neither
family had any previous record of genius. But parents and son
together experienced the impact of most of the forces – political,
economic, religious, and esthetic – from the Act of Union at the
beginning of the eighteenth century to the French Revolution at
the end, which changed Scotland from a proud, half-feudal, half-
theocratic kingdom to a mere English colony frequently called
'North Britain.' To understand Burns one must remember the
history of his country, and especially its literature.

Lowland Scots was not a provincial speech; it was a separate
language deriving from the Northumbrian dialect of Old English,
and bearing much the same relation to Southern English that
Catalan bears to Spanish. In the later Middle Ages and the
earlier Renaissance, Scots poetry was a formidable rival of English. In fact, in the century and a half between the death of
Chaucer and the accession of Queen Elizabeth, England produced
no poet as good as Robert Henryson (fl. 1480), William Dunbar
(d. 1520), Gavin Douglas (d. 1522), or David Lindsay (d. 1555).
At the beginning of the sixteenth century Scotland had reason to
expect a flowering of poetry comparable to the age of Shakespeare

---

*William Burnes and most of his kinfolk on the East Coast—he was born
in Kincardineshire—usually spelt the name as 'Burnes' or 'Burness'
and presumably pronounced it as two syllables. The poet signed himself
'Burness' in a few of his early letters, but soon settled on 'Burns,'
perhaps because it was easier to rhyme.

in the southern kingdom. Politics and religion combined to thwart humanistic hopes.

The Reformation, under the dynamic leadership of John Knox, took a particularly virulent form in Scotland. Like his master Calvin, Knox sought to create a theocratic state so omnipotent that Milton later said that 'new Presbyter is but old Priest writ large.' To Knox the grimmest rigors of the Massachusetts Colony would have seemed reprehensible laxness. The Scottish Inquisition operated on the parochial, not the national level, and lacked power to relax convicted heretics to the secular arm. Otherwise it strongly resembled its Spanish prototype. The Calvinist philosophy had the doctrinal rigidity of orthodox Marxism, plus a general Puritan condemnation of secular amusements, including music and dancing. What could not be destroyed was driven underground. One of the Reformation's greatest injuries to Scottish literature, however, was inadvertent.

All the branches of nascent Protestantism stressed the individual's need for knowledge of the Bible in his own tongue. Knox and his followers adopted the Geneva translation of 1560 as more consonant with their doctrine than the Anglican Bishops' Bible. But the Geneva, like all the others, was in standard Southern English. Hence the Scots willy-nilly conducted their public worship and private devotions in a dialect different from their daily speech. Though their pronunciation was Scottish, the spelling and idioms were English, and perhaps suggested that the Southern tongue was somehow holier than the Northern.

But it was politics, not religion, that struck the final blow at Scots as a literary language. On the death of Queen Elizabeth in 1603, James VI of Scotland became James I of England and lost no time in transferring his court from bleak and turbulent Edinburgh to richer and more salubrious London. There his Scottish courtiers found themselves ridiculed for their provincial speech – a whole generation later Milton pretended that the simple name 'Gillespie' was too uncouth to pronounce – and set about anglicizing themselves. They were still working at it to Boswell's day.

By that time, though, Scotland as a nation had ceased to exist. The Act of Union in 1707 had abolished the Scottish Parliament; the Act of Settlement of 1701 had abolished the Stuart dynasty – Scotland's own sovereigns, even though absentee – in favor of the House of Hanover, privately described by Burns as 'an obscure beef-witted insolent race of foreigners whom a con-

juncture of circumstances kickt up into power and consequence.'
In the Highlands loyalty to the deposed Stuarts survived for a
few years, oftener in words than in deeds. The Old Pretender,
Prince James, in 1715, and his son, Prince Charles Edward, in
1745, tried to raise rebellion, and succeeded only in bringing the
best of their followers to exile or the scaffold.

After Charles Edward's effort was crushed on the moor at
Culloden the English authorities saw to it that the Highlands
could never rebel again. The Duke of Cumberland's troops
carried arson, slaughter, and rape into the remotest glens, and
followed that purge with a series of penal laws which utterly
disarmed the clansmen and even forbade the wearing of the
tartan kilt. Such of the chieftains as had backed King George or
had waited on the fence found it easy to transform themselves
from feudal magnates to rack-renting and often absentee landlords. The Highland and Hebrides world which Johnson and
Boswell encountered in 1773 was a scant generation old.

The breaking of the Highlands was accomplished by force, and
from without. During the same decades the Lowlands were
largely transformed from within. The Union had admitted
Scottish commerce to the full privileges of the Navigation Act.
By the middle of the century the West Coast ports, Glasgow in
particular, had developed a thriving trade with the American
colonies and the West Indies; Scots also infiltrated the East
India Company. From these ventures many of the survivors
returned with substantial fortunes, and started an inflationary
spiral. Landed property was a safe investment; more important,
it was the pre-eminent symbol of status. The nabob's presence in
the countryside, in Macaulay's terse phrase, raised the price of
everything from fresh eggs to rotten boroughs. Then the nabobs,
to get an adequate return on their capital, increased their rents
and tried to bring marginal land into cultivation. Small tenant
farmers like William Burnes were caught between the millstones,
and grew poorer as their landlords grew richer.

The consequences of the Union were not limited to politics and
trade. Scotland, torn by theological controversy and civil war,
had not kept intellectual pace with England in the seventeenth
century. While the Southern kingdom, stimulated by Isaac
Newton, the Royal Society, and the dawning of the Enlightenment, was becoming the intellectual leader of Europe, Scotland
was still debating Calvinism. But the Enlightenment was one of
the invisible imports which accompanied Scotland's widening

intercourse with the outside world. By the third quarter of the eighteenth century, Scotland, at such impressive hands as Adam Smith's and David Hume's, was exporting ideas as well as whisky.

By mid-century the rationalism of the Enlightenment had even begun to infect the Kirk. Some of the younger clergy, in defiance of Knox and Calvin, sought – the phrase again is Burns's – 'to give a decent character to Almighty God and a rational account of his proceedings with the Sons of Men' by leavening their discourse with 'natural' religion. This doctrine was congenial to many of the more liberal-minded laity who had the right to nominate parish ministers. The orthodox or 'Old Light' Calvinists, both clerical and lay, fiercely counterattacked the 'New Light' heresy. By the time Burns reached manhood, half the parishes in Ayrshire were ululating with charges and countercharges.

II

With expanding intellectual horizons came antiquarian interest in Scotland's Chaucerian and Renaissance poets. Selections of their works were reprinted, sometimes with modernized spelling; ballads and folksongs began to be collected. The most prominent of the earlier editors was Allan Ramsay (1686–1758), poet and antiquary. In the latter capacity he edited *The Ever Green* (1724), an anthology of the older poetry, and *The Tea-Table Miscellany* (1724 ff.), a collection of ballads and songs, some of them really old, some reworked from old originals, some the work of Ramsay himself and his friends. He defended his own use of Scotticisms, in terms subsequently echoed by Burns, and established the convention that his readers were too refined to understand the 'Doric' without glossarial aid.

Herein lies the difference between the Scottish poetry of the eighteenth century and that of the earlier 'makars' – Dunbar and the rest. These used the Scots vernacular because it was their native tongue, which they felt no compulsion to apologize for. But for Ramsay, and after him Fergusson and Burns, 'standard' literature meant Southern English from Shakespeare to Pope. (Dryden was just as confident of his ability to 'improve' Chaucer as Ramsay was of his to remodel old songs.) When they wrote Scots they did so by conscious choice, as Lowell used Down East Yankee, and for the same reason – you could, under the guise of humor, get away with opinions that might make trouble if stated solemnly. Robert Burns, born in 1759, was in his twenties before he realized that the vernacular was still capable of serious literary use.

His formal education was scanty to the point of non-existence – two years, 1765–6, at John Murdoch's school; three special terms, widely spaced from 1772 to 1775. The curriculum was based wholly on standard English; if Scottish writers were acknowledged it was in the securely anglicized persons of James Thomson of *The Seasons* and John Home of *The Tragedy of Douglas.* A longer exposure to such schooling might well have fenced Burns completely away from his native traditions. As it was, his readings in Southern English account for much of his weakest verse.

There was a mawkish element in his nature which responded too readily to the second-best. He read Addison, Shenstone, and Young rather than Swift and Johnson. Above all, he delighted in Henry Mackenzie's maudlin *Man of Feeling* in preference to Fielding and Smollett. He even tried to be a 'Man of Feeling' himself, describing himself – in a phrase borrowed from Mackenzie – as 'not formed for the bustle of the busy nor the flutter of the gay.' In a similar mood of belated adolescent yeastiness in 1783 he began a folio commonplace book, announcing himself on the title page as 'a man of some sense, a great deal of honesty and unbounded goodwill' though 'bred at the plough-tail,' and buttressing this carefully posed outburst of modesty with a couple of appropriate quotations from Shenstone.

The opening leaves of the manuscript are worthy of the title page – turgid declamations from unnamed and unwritten tragedies, a self-conscious 'critical' analysis of his first attempt at song writing, a prose passage in which he avows that his leisure hours are spent with 'Ossian, Shakespeare, Thomson, Shenstone, Sterne, &c.' Such entries continue until September, 1784. Under that date appear two songs, 'O Tibby, I hae seen the day' and the arrant bawdy which begins, 'My girl she's airy.' After that there are no entries for seven months.

When they resume, their character has changed. First comes a rousing recension of the old ballad of John Barleycorn; next, a burlesque – the speaker is a sheep – of the traditional 'death and dying words' type of ballad; then a couple of poetic epistles in broad Scots. Burns for the first time had encountered the poems of Robert Fergusson, the Edinburgh law clerk who a decade before had died in the madhouse. The discovery electrified him as Chapman's Homer did Keats. In his own phrase, Fergusson roused him 'to emulating vigor.' Here was no rustic, speaking an obsolete and uncouth dialect out of pure ignorance; this was an educated son of the Athens of the North, writing descriptions, satires, and epistles as if James Thomson and Henry Mackenzie had never existed, even daring to poke fun at the latter in verses entitled 'The Sow of Feeling.' Burns realized suddenly that Ayrshire offered as many themes for sentiment and satire as Edinburgh did. His 'emulating vigor' included direct imitation: 'Brigs of Ayr,' for instance, parallels 'The Plainstanes and the Causey'; 'The Cotter's Saturday Night' imitates but is inferior to 'The Farmer's Ingle.' Mainly, however, Fergusson influenced by suggestion rather than direct borrowing.

In Mauchline, the Auld Lichts and the New Lichts were squabbling furiously, and what had begun as doctrinal dispute was rapidly sinking into personal feuding. Burns's landlord, Gavin Hamilton, was, like Burns himself, a free-thinker. One of the Auld Licht elders, Willie Fisher, had Hamilton arraigned before the Kirk Session on a charge of Sabbath-breaking – he had ordered a servant to dig new potatoes on Sunday. Hamilton, instead of submitting meekly, appealed his case to the Presbytery of Ayr, and won it. Burns celebrated the victory by writing 'Holy Willie's Prayer,' that matchless parody of Calvinist devotion. Along with 'The Ordination,' 'The Holy Fair,' and the 'Address to the Deil,' it dealt a body blow from which in the long view orthodoxy never quite recovered. In the short view, though, Burns had made Mauchline too hot to live in.

His amatory prowess, of course, added to the scandal – but it is needless to rehearse here his contributions to vital statistics (see the Chronology which follows). Early in 1786 he had the offer of a clerkship in Jamaica; before sailing, he determined to publish his poems – not, as is often stated, to pay his passage, but as a memento for his friends and a last fling at his enemies. The unexpected success of his Kilmarnock collection issued at the end of July, ended all thought of emigration. But the 'emulating vigor' inspired by Fergusson had spent itself. Though he would continue to write occasional epistles and satires, the verve of the work of 1784–1786 was lacking. Yet the second phase of his genius – as a lyricist – had scarcely begun.

The Kirk had failed utterly in its efforts to suppress dancing and secular music. Hundreds of ballads and songs still circulated orally, each with its own tune; other hundreds of airs for fiddle or bagpipes lacked words or had only bawdy ones. Burns was passionately fond of this music (his first poem, 'Handsome Nell,' was a song), but had no idea that scholars and antiquarians were seriously studying it. Not until the spring of 1787, near the end of his first sojourn in Edinburgh, did he meet James Johnson, a music engraver who was compiling *The Scots Musical Museum*. He aimed to collect all the extant Scottish songs and airs. Burns threw himself into the work with enthusiasm and with knowledge far surpassing Johnson's. He became in fact, though not in title, the *Museum*'s chief editor. For it, and for George Thomson's *Select Collection of Scottish Airs*, he composed or compiled more than three hundred songs. Some were wholly his own; some were improvised from fragments of old choruses; some were wholly traditional. But on internal evidence alone it is seldom possible to be sure which is which. He disclaimed the authorship of 'Auld Lang Syne,' though no earlier recording of it has ever been found. He tacitly claimed 'A Red, Red Rose' and rightly, though every stanza has been traced to older originals. With the aid of music – every one of his lyrics was written to a specific tune – he could, without condescension, *think* in folk speech.

He was quite aware of what he was doing, and admitted that knowledge of both Scots and English gave him a richer and more flexible medium than either dialect was capable of alone. Thus he could alternate between the tongues as the exigencies of rhyme and metre indicated. But his stance between the worlds was precarious enough. Though he had every trick of the popular ballad at his fingertips, he could not write a serious ballad, and used the form only for satire or burlesque. Born a generation later, the inhibiting sophistication might have checked his song-writing also. His place in Scottish literature was the point of no return.

Even 'Tam O' Shanter,' his masterpiece, shows this double vision. It is a humorous retelling of a Scottish folktale; it is also a superb and conscious work of art. Its unique blend of comedy and terror was possible only in a world where belief in witch-craft was not yet wholly extinct. Burns did not believe in witches, but he had grown up among people who did. Thus 'Tam,' like the rest of Burns's work, is rooted in Scotland's past, not in her present or future. To classify him as a forerunner of the Romantic movement is completely to misunderstand him and the world he lived in. The writers of 'sensibility' influenced him to his detriment; his robust realism, his earthy and often bawdy humor had no reciprocal influence on them.

In the present century fervid Scottish nationalists have tried to revive 'Lallans' (Lowlands) as a poetic medium. The results have not been spectacular. Poetry bred under glass is not hardy in the stern and wild climate of Caledonia. One contemporary, Maurice Lindsay, after preaching it and practicing it for twenty years, declared recently that Lallans is an anachronism. There have been great Scottish writers since Burns; there have been no great writers of Scots.

In selecting the poems for this edition the editor has endeavored to choose those verses which most directly link Burns to the great tradition of Scottish poetry. This has meant the exclusion of practically all of Burns's efforts at standard English, as well as of verses deriving from such contemporary works as 'The Man of Feeling.' It also accounts for the omission of 'The Cotter's Saturday Night,' 'The Haggis,' and one or two other poems that are traditionally included.

The best complete edition of Burns's *Poems* is still the Centenary, edited by William Ernest Henley and T. F. Henderson, published in Edinburgh, 1896. The present selections follow the Centenary throughout; the glossarial notes have been revised.

DELANCEY FERGUSON

Falls Village, Connecticut

CHRONOLOGY OF
THE LIFE OF BURNS

I. AYRSHIRE

1759　JANUARY 25. Robert Burns born at Alloway; eldest son of William Burnes (1721–1784) and his wife Agnes Broun (1732–1820). The other children were Gilbert (1760–1827), Agnes (1762–1834), Anabella (1764–1832), William (1767–1790), John (1769–1785), and Isabella (1771–1858).

1765　Robert and Gilbert sent to school to John Murdoch.

1766　William Burnes rents Mt. Oliphant farm.

1772　Robert and Gilbert attend Dalrymple parish school, in alternate weeks, during summer quarter.

1773　Robert studies grammar and French with Murdoch for three weeks; writes his first song, 'Handsome Nell,' for Nellie Kilpatrick.

1775　Burns attends Hugh Rodger's school at Kirkoswald.

1777　The Burns family moves to Lochlie farm, near Tarbolton.

1783　APRIL. Burns begins his Commonplace Book.
　　　AUTUMN. Robert and Gilbert arrange to rent Mossgiel farm from Gavin Hamilton of Mauchline.

1784　FEBRUARY 13. Death of William Burnes. The family moves to Mossgiel.

1785　MAY 22. Birth of Elizabeth, the poet's daughter by Elizabeth Paton, a farm servant.
　　　During this year Burns begins to write his satires, composes 'The Jolly Beggars,' and in October finishes his first Commonplace Book.
　　　AUTUMN. Burns's love affair with Jean Armour begins.

1786　JANUARY (?). Burns plans migration to Jamaica.
　　　APRIL 3. 'Proposals' for the Kilmarnock *Poems* sent to press.
　　　APRIL. Burns offers marriage to Jean Armour, four months pregnant; her father refuses assent. Burns turns his attention to Mary Campbell ('Highland Mary').
　　　MAY 14. Supposed date of farewell to Highland Mary.

1786   JULY 9. By submitting to public rebuke for fornication, Burns voids his previous offer of marriage.

JULY 22. Burns transfers his share in Mossgiel to Gilbert.

JULY 31. The Kilmarnock *Poems* published.

c. SEPTEMBER 1. First postponement of Jamaica voyage.

SEPTEMBER 3. Jean Armour bears twins, who are christened Robert and Jean.

c. SEPTEMBER 27. Second postponement of Jamaica voyage.

END OF OCTOBER. Abandonment of Jamaica plans.

DECEMBER 1. On the success of the Kilmarnock Edition, Elizabeth Paton had threatened suit against Burns. The claim was settled on his payment of twenty pounds and his agreement to assume all expenses for his daughter's rearing.

II. EDINBURGH

1786   NOVEMBER 29. Burns arrives in Edinburgh.

DECEMBER 9. Henry Mackenzie praises the Kilmarnock *Poems* in *The Lounger.*

DECEMBER 14. William Creech issues subscription bills for the Edinburgh edition of the *Poems.*

1787   JANUARY 13. The Grand Lodge of Scotland toasts Burns as 'Caledonia's Bard.'

APRIL 21. Edinburgh *Poems* published.

MAY 5–JUNE 1. Burns tours the Border.

END OF MAY. Volume I of Johnson's *Scots Musical Museum* published.

JUNE 8. Burns's 'éclatant return to Mauchline.'

JULY 29. Jean Armour 'in for it again.'

AUGUST 15. Burns sued by Meg Cameron, an Edinburgh servant girl.

AUGUST 25–SEPTEMBER 16. Highland tour with William Nicol, teacher of Latin in Edinburgh High School.

DECEMBER 4. Burns meets Agnes M'Lehose, a sentimental lady living apart from her husband.

DECEMBER 8. At Mrs. M'Lehose's suggestion they start a correspondence, using pastoral pen-names, 'Clarinda' and 'Sylvander.'

1788   MARCH 3. Jean Armour bears twin girls, who die shortly after.

MARCH 18. Burns signs lease of Ellisland Farm, near Dumfries.

MARCH. Volume II of *Scots Musical Museum* published.

APRIL. Burns acknowledges Jean Armour as his wife.

APRIL–MAY. Burns takes training course at Mauchline to qualify for the Excise service.

III. DUMFRIESSHIRE

1788 JUNE 11. Burns settles at Ellisland.
JULY 14. Burns's Excise commission issued.
NOVEMBER. Jenny Clow, another Edinburgh servant girl, bears Burns a son.

1789 SUMMER. Burns meets Francis Grose, an antiquary compiling the history of *Antiquities of Scotland*.
SEPTEMBER 1. Burns begins duty as Excise officer.

1790 FEBRUARY. Volume III of *Scots Musical Museum* published.
JULY. Burns transferred to a Dumfries division of the Excise.
DECEMBER 1. Ms. of 'Tam o' Shanter' sent to Grose.

1791 MARCH 31. Anne Park, a Dumfries barmaid, bears Burns a daughter, Elizabeth.
APRIL. 'Tam o' Shanter' published in Grose's *Antiquities of Scotland* and in the March *Edinburgh Magazine*.
SEPTEMBER 10. Formal renunciation of Ellisland lease signed.
NOVEMBER 11. Burns moves into Dumfries.

1792 FEBRUARY. Burns promoted to Dumfries Port Division.
AUGUST. Volume IV of *Scots Musical Museum* published.
SEPTEMBER 16. Burns begins work for Thomson's *Select Collection*.
DECEMBER 31. Official inquiry into Burns's alleged support of the French Revolution.

1793 FEBRUARY. Second Edinburgh edition of *Poems* published.
MARCH. Burns, an honorary burgess, petitions for full burgess privileges in the schools. Petition is granted.
JUNE. First number of Thomson's *Select Collection of Scottish Airs* published.

1794 *c.* DECEMBER 22. Burns appointed Acting Supervisor at Dumfries.

1795 DECEMBER–JANUARY. Burns ill with rheumatic fever.

1796 JULY 21. Death of Burns.

TABLE OF CONTENTS

APPENDIX

PART ONE
SATIRES AND EPISTLES

THE TWA DOGS

A Tale

'Twas in that place o' Scotland's isle
That bears the name of auld King Coil,†   Kẏle (central district
                                             of Ayrshire)
Upon a bonie day in June,
When wearing thro' the afternoon,
Twa†dogs, that were na thrang†at hame,   two; busy
Forgathered†ance upon a time.   chance-met

The first I'll name, they ca'd him Caesar,
Was keepit for 'his Honor's' pleasure:
His hair, his size, his mouth, his lugs,†   ears
Shew'd he was nane o' Scotland's dogs;
But whalpit†some place far abroad,   whelped
Whare sailors gang to fish for cod.

His lockèd, letter'd, braw brass collar
Shew'd him the gentleman an' scholar;
But tho' he was o' high degree,
The fient a†pride, nae pride had he;   devil a (not any)
But wad hae spent an hour caressin,
Ev'n wi' a tinkler-gipsy's messin;†   mongrel

At kirk or market, mill or smiddie,†   smithy
Nae tawted tyke,† tho' e'er sae duddie,†   matted cur; ragged
But he wad stan't,† as glad to see him,   would have stood
An' stroan't†on stanes an' hillocks wi' him.   pissed

The tither was a ploughman's collie,
rollicking; blade   A rhyming, ranting,[†] raving billie,[†]
Wha for his friend an' comrade had him,
And in his freaks had Luath ca'd him,
After some dog in Highland sang,
Was made lang syne – Lord knows how lang.

wise   He was a gash[†]an' faithfu' tyke,
ditch; stone fence   As ever lap a sheugh[†]or dyke.[†]
pleasant; white-streaked   His honest, sonsie,[†] baws'nt[†]face
every   Ay gat him friends in ilka[†]place;
shaggy   His breast was white, his tousie[†]back
Weel clad wi' coat o' glossy black;
joyous   His gawsie[†]tail, wi' upward curl,
buttocks   Hung owre his hurdies[†]wi' a swirl.

glad   Nae doubt but they were fain[†]o' ither,
confidential   And unco pack an' thick[†]thegither;
now   Wi' social nose whyles[†]snuff'd an' snowkit;
moles; dug   Whyles mice an' moudieworts[†]they howkit;[†]
Whyles scour'd awa' in lang excursion,
An' worry'd ither in diversion;
Till tir'd at last wi' monie a farce,
They sat them down upon their arse,
An' there began a lang digression
About the 'lords o' the creation.'

CAESAR

I've aften wonder'd, honest Luath,
What sort o' life poor dogs like you have;
An' when the gentry's life I saw,
at all   What way poor bodies liv'd ava.[†]

Our laird gets in his rackèd rents,
rents in kind; dues   His coals, his kain,[†] an' a' his stents:[†]
He rises when he likes himsel;
His flunkies answer at the bell;
He ca's his coach; he ca's his horse;
He draws a bonie silken purse,
stitches   As lang's my tail, whare, thro' the steeks,[†]
guinea coin; peeps   The yellow letter'd Geordie[†]keeks.[†]

Frae morn to e'en it's nought but toiling,
At baking, roasting, frying, boiling;
An' tho' the gentry first are stechin,[†]   cramming
Yet ev'n the ha' folk[†]fill their pechan[†]   servants; stomach
Wi' sauce, ragouts, an sic like trashtrie,
That's little short o' downright wastrie:
Our whipper-in, wee, blastit wonner,[†]   wonder
Poor, worthless elf, it eats a dinner,
Better than onie tenant-man
His Honor has in a' the lan';
An' what poor cot-folk pit[†]their painch[†]in,   put; paunch
I own it's past my comprehension.

LUATH

Trowth, Caesar, whyles[†]they're fash't[†]eneugh: sometimes; bothered
A cotter howkin[†]in a sheugh,   digging
Wi' dirty stanes biggin[†]a dyke,   building
Baring[†]a quarry, an' sic like;   clearing
Himsel, a wife, he thus sustains,
A smytrie[†]o' wee duddie[†]weans,   litter; brats
An' nought but his han' darg[†]to keep   hands' labour
Them right an' tight in thack an' rape.[†]   thatch and rope

An' when they meet wi' sair disasters,
Like loss o' health or want o' masters,
Ye maist wad think, a wee[†]touch langer,   small
An' they maun starve o' cauld and hunger:
But how it comes, I never kend yet,
They're maistly wonderfu' contented;
An' buirdly chiels,[†] an' clever hizzies,[†]   stout lads;
Are bred in sic a way as this is.   young women

CAESAR

But then to see how ye're negleckit,
How huff'd, an' cuff'd, an' disrespeckit!
Lord man, our gentry care as little
For delvers, ditchers, an' sic cattle;
They gang as saucy by poor folk,
As I wad by a stinking brock.[†]   badger

[3]

I've notic'd, on our laird's court-day,
sad (An' monie a time my heart's been wae†),
Poor tenant bodies, scant o' cash,
endure; How they maun thole†a factor's snash:†
abuse He'll stamp an' threaten, curse an' swear
seize He'll apprehend them, poind†their gear;
stand While they maun staun',† wi' aspect humble,
An' hear it a', an' fear an' tremble!

I see how folk live that hae riches;
But surely poor-folk maun be wretches!

LUATH

They're nae sae wretched's ane wad think:
poverty's Tho' constantly on poortith's†brink,
They're sae accustom'd wi' the sight,
The view o't gies them little fright.

Then chance an' fortune are sae guided,
They're ay in less or mair provided;
An' tho' fatigu'd wi' close employment,
snatch A blink†o' rest's a sweet enjoyment.

The dearest comfort o' their lives,
growing Their grushie†weans an' faithfu' wives;
The prattling things are just their pride,
That sweetens a' their fire-side.

sometimes; An' whyles†twalpennie worth o' nappy†
ale Can mak the bodies unco happy:
They lay aside their private cares,
To mind the Kirk and State affairs;
They'll talk o' patronage an' priests,
Wi' kindling fury i' their breasts,
Or tell what new taxation's comin,
marvel An' ferlie†at the folk in Lon'on.

As bleak-fac'd Hallowmass returns,
harvest- They get the jovial, ranting kirns,†
homes When rural life, of ev'ry station,
Unite in common recreation;

Love blinks,[†] Wit slaps, an' social Mirth   glances
Forgets there's Care upo' the earth.

    That merry day the year begins,
They bar the door on frosty win's;
The nappy reeks wi' mantling ream,[†]   cream
An' sheds a heart-inspiring steam;
The luntin[†] pipe, an' sneeshin[†] mill,   smoking; snuff-box
Are handed round wi' right guid will;
The cantie auld folks crackin crouse,[†]   conversing cheerfully
The young anes ranting[†] thro' the house –   romping
My heart has been sae fain to see them,
That I for joy hae barkit wi' them.

    Still it's owre true that ye hae said
Sic game is now owre aften[†] play'd;   too often
There's monie a creditable stock
O' decent, honest, fawsont[†] folk,   well-doing
Are riven out baith root an' branch,
Some rascal's pridefu' greed to quench,
Wha thinks to knit himsel the faster
In favor wi' some gentle master,
Wha, aiblins[†] thrang a parliamentin',   may be
For Britain's guid his saul indentin'[†] –   indenturing

    Haith, lad, ye little ken about it:
For Britain's guid! guid faith! I doubt it.
Say rather, gaun[†] as Premiers lead him: going
An' saying aye or no's they bid him:
At operas an' plays parading,
Mortgaging, gambling, masquerading:
Or maybe, in a frolic daft,
To Hague or Calais taks a waft,
To mak a tour an' tak a whirl,
To learn *bon ton*, an' see the worl'.

    There, at Vienna or Versailles,
He rives[†] his father's auld entails;   splits
Or by Madrid he taks the rout,[†]   road
To thrum guitars an' fecht[†] wi' nowt;[†]   fight; cattle
Or down Italian vista[†] startles,   courses
Whore-hunting amang groves o' myrtles

muddy

Then bowses drumlie†German-water,
To mak himsel look fair an' fatter,
An' clear the consequential sorrows,
Love-gifts of Carnival signoras.

For Britain's guid! for her destruction!
Wi' dissipation, feud an' faction.

way

Hech man! dear sirs! is that the gate†
They waste sae monie a braw estate!

troubled

Are we sae foughten†an' harass'd

wealth to go

For gear ta gang†that gate at last?

O would they stay aback frae courts,
An' please themsels wi' countra sports,
It wad for ev'ry ane be better,
The laird, the tenant, an' the cotter!

those; roistering

For thae†frank, rantin,† ramblin billies,

Devil a one

Fient haet†o' them's ill-hearted fellows:

wasting their woods

Except for breakin o' their timmer,†

mistress

Or speakin lightly o' their limmer,†
Or shootin of a hare or moor-cock,
The ne'er-a-bit they're ill to poor folk.

But will ye tell me, master Caesar:
Sure great folk's life's a life o' pleasure?

touch

Nae cauld nor hunger e'er can steer†them,
The vera thought o't need na fear them.

Lord, man, were ye but whyles whare I am,
The gentles, ye wad ne'er envý 'em!

It's true, they need na starve or sweat,
Thro' winter's cauld, or simmer's heat;

hard

They've nae sair†wark to craze their banes,

gripes and groans

An' fill auld-age wi' grips an' granes:†
But human bodies are sic fools,
For a' their colleges an' schools,

That when nae real ills perplex them,
They mak enow themsels to vex them;
An' ay the less they hae to sturt†them,   fret
In like proportion, less will hurt them.

    A countra fellow at the pleugh,
His acre's till'd, he's right eneugh;
A countra girl at her wheel,
Her dizzen's†done, she's unco weel;   dozen
But gentlemen, an' ladies warst,
Wi' ev'n down†want o' wark are curst: positive
They loiter, lounging, lank an' lazy;
Tho' deil-haet†ails them, yet uneasy: nothing
Their days insipid, dull an' tasteless;
Their nights unquiet, lang an' restless.

    An' ev'n their sports, their balls an' races,
Their galloping through public places,
There's sic parade, sic pomp an' art,
The joy can scarcely reach the heart.

    The men cast out in party-matches,
Then sowther†a' in deep debauches;   solder
Ae†night they're mad wi' drink an' whoring, One
Niest†day their life is past enduring.   Next

    The ladies arm-in-arm in clusters,
As great an' gracious a' as sisters;
But hear their absent thoughts o' ither,
They're a' run†deils an' jads†thegither. downright; jades
Whyles, owre the wee bit cup an' platie,
They sip the scandal-potion pretty;
Or lee-lang†nights, wi' crabbit leuks   live-long
Pore owre the devil's pictur'd beuks;†   books
                               (playing cards)
Stake on a chance a farmer's stackyard,
An' cheat like onie unhang'd blackguard.

    There's some exceptions, man an' woman;
But this is Gentry's life in common.

    By this, the sun was out o' sight,
An' darker gloamin†brought the night;   twilight
The bum-clock†humm'd wi' lazy drone;   beetle
The kye†stood rowtin†i' the loan;†   cattle; lowing; lane

[7]

ears   When up they gat, an' shook their lugs,†
Rejoic'd they were na *men*, but *dogs*;
An' each took aff his several way,
Resolv'd to meet some ither day.

SCOTCH DRINK

Gie him strong drink until he wink,
That's sinking in despair;
An' liquor guid to fire his bluid,
That's prest wi' grief an' care:
There let him bowse, and deep carouse,
Wi' bumpers fiowing o'er,
Till he forgets his loves or debts,
An' minds his griefs no more.

SOLOMON'S PROVERBS, xxxi. 6, 7

1

Let other poets raise a frácas
'Bout vines, an' wines, an' drucken Bacchus,

torment   An' crabbit names an' stories wrack†us,
vex; ear   An' grate†our lug:†
barley   I sing the juice Scotch bear†can mak us,
                  In glass or jug.

2

coils of a   O thou, my Muse! guid auld Scotch drink!
   still; frisk   Whether thro' wimplin worms†thou jink,†
cream   Or, richly brown, ream†owre the brink,
foam   In glorious faem,†
Inspire me, till I lisp an' wink,
                  To sing thy name!

3

hollows   Let husky wheat the haughs†adorn,
oats;   An' aits†set up their awnie†horn,
   bearded   An' pease an' beans, at e'en or morn,
                  Perfume the plain:
Blessings on   Leeze me on thee,† John Barleycorn,
   thee   Thou king o' grain!

4

On thee aft Scotland chows her cood,
In souple[†] scones, the wale[†] o' food!   tender; pick
Or tumbling in the boiling flood
    Wi' kail[†] an' beef;   greens
But when thou pours thy strong heart's blood,[†] whisky
    There thou shines chief.

5

Food fills the wame,[†] an' keeps us livin; belly
Tho' life's a gift no worth receivin,
When heavy-dragg'd wi' pine an' grievin;
    But oil'd by thee,
The wheels o' life gae down-hill, scrievin,[†] careering
    Wi' rattlin glee.

6

Thou clears the head o' doited Lear,[†]   muddled
Thou cheers the heart o' drooping Care; Learning
Thou strings the nerves o' Labour sair,
    At's weary toil;
Thou ev'n brightens dark Despair
    Wi' gloomy smile.

7

Aft, clad in massy siller weed,[†]   dress
Wi' gentles[†] thou erects thy head;   gentry
Yet, humbly kind in time o' need,
    The poor man's wine:
His wee drap parritch,[†] or his bread, porridge
    Thou kitchens[†] fine.   seasons

8

Thou art the life o' public haunts:
But[†] thee, what were our fairs and rants?[†] Without;
Ev'n godly meetings o' the saunts,   merry-
    By thee inspir'd,   makings
When, gaping, they besiege the tents,
    Are doubly fir'd.

9

That merry night we get the corn in,
O sweetly, then, thou reams the horn in!
Or reekin[†] on a New-Year mornin smoking
    In cog or bicker,[†]   mug or cup
An' just a wee drap sp'ritual[†] burn in, whisky
    An' gusty sucker![†] tasty sugar

10

When Vulcan gies his bellows breath,
gear   An' ploughmen gather wi' their graith,[†]
froth   O rare! to see thee fizz an' freath[†]
two-eared cup   I' th' lugget caup![†]
the Blacksmith   Then Burnewin[†]comes on like death
stroke   At ev'ry chaup.[†]

11

Nae mercy, then, for airn or steel:
bony; fellow   The brawnie, bainie,[†] ploughman chiel,[†]
Brings hard owrehip, wi' sturdy wheel,
     The strong forehammer,
anvil   Till block an' studdie[†]ring an' reel,
     Wi' dinsome clamor.

12

squalling babies   When skirlin weanies[†]see the light,
babble cheerfully   Thou maks the gossips clatter bright,[†]
dolts   How fumbling cuifs[†]their dearies slight;
Woe befall   Wae worth[†]the name!
midwife   Nae howdie[†]gets a social night,
coin   Or plack[†]frae them.

13

law-case   When neebors anger at a plea,[†]
wild   An' just as wud[†]as wud can be,
-brew   How easy can the barley-brie[†]
     Cement the quarrel!
It's aye the cheapest lawyer's fee,
     To taste the barrel.

14

Alake! that e'er my Muse has reason,
charge   To wyte[†]her countrymen wi' treason!
throats   But monie daily weet their weason[†]
     Wi' liquors nice,
An' hardly, in a winter season,
ask   E'er spier[†]her price.

15

Wae worth that brandy, burnin trash!
illness   Fell source o' monie a pain an' brash![†]
robs; stupid;   Twins[†]monie a poor, doylt,[†] drucken hash,[†]
  drunken oaf   O' half his days;
An' sends, beside, auld Scotland's cash
     To her warst faes.

16

Ye Scots, wha wish auld Scotland well!
Ye chief, to you my tale I tell,
Poor, plackless⁺devils like mysel!   penniless
            It sets⁺you ill,   becomes
Wi' bitter, dearthfu' wines to mell,⁺   meddle
            Or foreign gill.

17

May gravels round his blather⁺wrench,   bladder
An' gouts torment him, inch by inch,
Wha twists his gruntle⁺wi' a glunch⁺   snout; growl
            O' sour disdain,
Out owre a glass o' whisky-punch
            Wi' honest men!

18

O Whisky! soul o' plays an' pranks!
Accept a Bardie's gratefu' thanks!
When wanting thee, what tuneless cranks⁺   creakings
            Are my poor verses!
Thou comes – they rattle i' their ranks
            At ither's arses!

19

Thee, Ferintosh! O sadly lost!
Scotland lament frae coast to coast!
Now colic grips, an' barkin hoast⁺   cough
            May kill us a';
For loyal Forbés' chartered boast
            Is taen awa!

20

Thae⁺curst horse-leeches o' th' Excise,   Those
Wha mak the whisky stells⁺their prize!   stills
Haud up thy han', Deil! ance, twice, thrice!
            There, seize the blinkers!⁺   spies
An' bake them up in brunstane pies
            For poor damn'd drinkers.

21

Fortune! if thou'll but gie me still
Hale breeks,⁺ a scone, an' whisky gill,   Whole breeches
An' rowth⁺o' rhyme to rave at will,   store
            Tak a' the rest,
An' deal't about as thy blind skill
            Directs thee best.

THE HOLY FAIR

A robe of seeming truth and trust
Hid crafty observation ;
And secret hung, with poison'd crust,
The dirk of defamation :
A mask that like the gorget show'd,
Dye-varying on the pigeon ;
And for a mantle large and broad,
He wrapt him in Religion.

HYPOCRISY À-LA-MODE

1

Upon a simmer Sunday morn,
   When Nature's face is fair,
I walkèd forth to view the corn,
   An' snuff the caller[†]air.
The rising sun, owre Galston Muirs,
   Wi' glorious light was glintin;[†]
The hares were hirplin[†]down the furs,[†]
   The lav'rocks[†]they were chantin
          Fu' sweet that day.

2

As lightsomely I glowr'd[†]abroad,
   To see a scene sae gay,
Three hizzies,[†] early at the road,
   Cam skelpin[†]up the way.
Twa had manteeles o' dolefu' black,
   But ane wi' lyart[†]lining;
The third, that gaed a wee a-back,[†]
   Was in the fashion shining
          Fu' gay that day.

Glosses (left margin):
cool
glancing
hopping; furrows
larks
gazed
young women
skipping
grey
walked a bit
   behind

[12]

The twa appear'd like sisters twin,
   In feature, form, an' claes;†   *clothes*
Their visage wither'd, lang an' thin,
   An' sour as onie slaes:†   *wild plums*
The third cam up, hap†-step-an'-lowp,†   *hop; jump*
   As light as onie lambie,
An' wi' a curchie†low did stoop,   *curtsy*
   As soon as e'er she saw me,
          Fu' kind that day.

4

Wi' bonnet aff, quoth I, 'Sweet lass,
   I think ye seem to ken me;
I'm sure I've seen that bonie face,
   But yet I canna name ye,'
Quo' she, an' laughin as she spak,
   An' taks me by the han's,
' Ye, for my sake, hae gi'en the feck†   *bulk*
   Of a' the Ten Comman's
          A screed†some day.   *rip*

5

'My name is Fun – your cronie dear,
   The nearest friend ye hae;
An' this is Superstition here,
   An' that's Hypocrisy.
I'm gaun†to Mauchline Holy Fair,   *going*
   To spend an hour in daffin:†   *larking*
Gin ye'll go there, yon runkl'd†pair,   *wrinkled*
   We will get famous laughin
          At them this day.'

6

Quoth I, 'Wi' a' my heart, I'll do't;
   I'll get my Sunday's sark†on,   *shirt*
An' meet you on the holy spot;
   Faith, we'se†hae fine remarkin!'   *we'll*
Then I gaed†hame at crowdie†-time,   *went; porridge-*
   An' soon I made me ready;
For roads were clad,† frae side to side,   *crowded*
   Wi' monie a wearie body,
          In droves that day.

7

self-complacent; gear   Here farmers gash,† in ridin graith,†
jogging   Gaed hoddin†by their cotters;
strapping youngsters   There swankies young,† in braw braid-claith,
     Are springin owre the gutters.
padding; thronging   The lasses, skelpin†barefit, thrang,†
     In silks an' scarlets glitter;
wedge   Wi' sweet-milk cheese, in monie a whang,†
small cakes   An' farls,† bak'd wi' butter,
crisp   Fu' crump†that day.

8

When by the plate we set our nose,
     Weel heapèd up wi' ha'pence,
the Elder   A greedy glowr black-bonnet†throws,
     An' we maun draw our tippence.
Then in we go to see the show:
     On ev'ry side they're gath'rin;
planks   Some carryin dails,† some chairs an' stools,
gabbling   An' some are busy bleth'rin†
       Right loud that day.

9

keep off   Here stands a shed to fend†the show'rs,
     An' screen our countra gentry;
two or three   There Racer Jess, an' twa-three†whores,
leering   Are blinkin†at the entry.
whispering jades   Here sits a raw o' tittlin jads,†
     Wi' heavin breasts an' bare neck;
weaver   An' there a batch o' wabster†lads,
     Blackguardin frae Kilmarnock,
       For fun this day.

10

Here some are thinkin on their sins,
     An' some upo' their claes;
soiled   Ane curses feet that fyl'd†his shins,
     Anither sighs an' prays:
sample   On this hand sits a chosen swatch,†
     Wi' screw'd-up, grace-proud faces;
On that a set o' chaps, at watch,
Busy   Thrang†winkin on the lasses
       To chairs that day.

11

O happy is that man an' blest!
   Nae wonder that it pride him!
Whase ain dear lass, that he likes best,
   Comes clinkin down beside him!
Wi' arm repos'd on the chair back,
   He sweetly does compose him;
Which, by degrees, slips round her neck,
   An's loof†upon her bosom,   And his palm
              Unkend that day.

12

Now a' the congregation o'er
   Is silent expectation;
For Moodie speels†the holy door,   opens
   Wi' tidings o' damnation:
Should Hornie,† as in ancient days,   the Devil
   'Mang sons o' God present him;
The vera sight o' Moodie's face
   To's ain het†hame had sent him   hot
              Wi' fright that day.

13

Hear how he clears the points o' Faith
   Wi' rattlin and thumpin!
Now meekly calm, now wild in wrath,
   He's stampin, an' he's jumpin!
His lengthen'd chin, his turn'd-up snout,
   His eldritch†squeel an' gestures,   unearthly
O how they fire the heart devout –
   Like cantharidian plaisters
             On sic a day!

14

But hark! the tent has chang'd its voice;
   There's peace an' rest nae langer;
For a' the real judges rise,
   They canna sit for anger:
Smith opens out his cauld harangues,
   On practice and on morals;
An' aff the godly pour in thrangs,
   To gie the jars an' barrels
            A lift that day.

15

What signifies his barren shine,
    Of moral pow'rs an' reason?
His English style, an' gesture fine
    Are a' clean out o' season.
Like Socrates or Antonine,
    Or some auld pagan heathen,
The moral man he does define,
    But ne'er a word o' faith in
            That's right that day.

16

In guid time comes an antidote
    Against sic poison'd nostrum;
river's mouth   For Peebles, frae the water-fit,[†]
    Ascends the holy rostrum:
See, up he's got the word o' God,
demurely   An' meek an' mim[†]has view'd it,
While Common-sense has taen the road,
    An' aff, an' up the Cowgate
            Fast, fast that day.

17

next   Wee Miller niest,[†] the guard relieves,
recites by rote   An' orthodoxy raibles,[†]
Tho' in his heart he weel believes,
    An' thinks it auld wives' fables:
fellow; living   But faith! the birkie[†]wants a manse:[†]
humbugs   So, cannilie he hums[†]them;
Altho' his carnal wit an' sense
Nearly half   Like hafflins-wise[†]o'ercomes him
            At times that day.

18

front and rear; tavern   Now butt an' ben[†]the change-house[†]fills,
ale-cup   Wi' yill-caup[†]commentators;
biscuits   Here's crying out for bakes[†]an' gills,
    An' there the pint-stowp clatters;
While thick an' thrang, an' loud an' lang,
    Wi' logic an' wi' Scripture,
They raise a din, that in the end
    Is like to breed a rupture
            O' wrath that day.

19

Leeze me on†drink! it gies us mair
   Than either school or college;
It kindles wit, it waukens lear,†
   It pangs†us fou o' knowledge:
Be't whisky-gill or penny wheep,†
   Or onie stronger potion,
It never fails, on drinkin deep,
   To kittle†up our notion,
         By night or day.

How I love

learning
crams
small beer

tickle

20

The lads an' lasses, blythely bent
   To mind baith saul an' body,
Sit round the table, weel content,
   An' steer†about the toddy:
On this ane's dress, an' that ane's leuk,
   They're makin observations;
While some are cozie i' the neuk,†
   An' formin assignations
         To meet some day.

stir

corner

21

But now the Lord's ain trumpet touts,†
   Till a' the hills are rairin,†
And echoes back return the shouts;
   Black Russell is na spairin:†
His piercin words, like Highlan' swords,
   Divide the joints an' marrow;
His talk o' Hell, whare devils dwell,
   Our verra 'sauls does harrow'
         Wi' fright that day!

sounds
roaring

sparing

22

A vast, unbottom'd, boundless pit,
   Fill'd fou†o' lowin†brunstane,
Whase ragin flame, an' scorchin heat,
   Wad melt the hardest whun-stane!
The half-asleep start up wi' fear,
   An' think they hear it roarin;
When presently it does appear,
   'Twas but some neebor snorin
         Asleep that day.

full; flaming

23

'Twad be owre lang a tale to tell,
  How monie stories past;
An' how they crouded to the yill,
  When they were a' dismist;

mugs; cups   How drink gaed round, in cogs[†]an' caups,[†]
  Amang the furms an' benches;
An' cheese an' bread, frae women's laps,

full portions   Was dealt about in lunches,[†]

lumps   An' dawds[†]that day.

24

jolly; sagacious   In comes a gawsie,[†] gash[†]guidwife,
  An' sits down by the fire,

Then; cheese   Syne[†]draws her kebbuck[†]an' her knife;
  The lasses they are shyer:
The auld guidmen, about the grace,
  Frae side to side they bother;
Till some ane by his bonnet lays,

rope   An' gies them't, like a tether,[†]
           Fu' lang that day.

25

Alas!   Waesucks![†]for him that gets nae lass,
  Or lasses that hae naething!
Sma' need has he to say a grace,

meal-dust   Or melvie[†]his braw claithing!
O wives, be mindfu', ance yoursel,
  How bonie lads ye wanted;
An' dinna for a kebbuck-heel
  Let lasses be affronted
         On sic a day!

26

the bell-ringer; rope   Now Clinkumbell,[†] wi' rattlin tow,[†]
swing and toll   Begins to jow an' croon;[†]
can   Some swagger hame the best they dow,[†]
  Some wait the afternoon.
openings; fellows; bit   At slaps[†]the billies[†]halt a blink,[†]
take off   Till lasses strip[†]their shoon:
Wi' faith an' hope, an' love an' drink,
  They're a' in famous tune
talk   For crack[†]that day.

How monie hearts this day converts
   O' sinners and o' lasses!
Their hearts o' stane, gin night,† are gane†   by nightfall;
   As saft as onie flesh is: gone
There's some are fou o' love divine;
   There's some are fou o' brandy;
An' monie jobs that day begin,
   May end in houghmagandie†   fornication
         Some ither day.

ADDRESS TO THE DEIL

O Prince! O Chief of many thronèd pow'rs!
That led th' embattl'd seraphim to war.
                MILTON

1

O Thou! whatever title suit thee –
Auld Hornie, Satan, Nick, or Clootie†–   Hoofie
Wha in yon cavern grim an' sootie,
         Clos'd under hatches,
Spairges†about the brunstane cootie,†   Splashes; dish
         To scaud†poor wretches! scald

2

Hear me, Auld Hangie,† for a wee,   Hangman
An' let poor damnèd bodies be;
I'm sure sma' pleasure it can gie,
         Ev'n to a deil,
To skelp†an' scaud poor dogs like me   spank
         An' hear us squeel.

3

Great is thy pow'r an' great thy fame;
Far kend an' noted is thy name;

flaming
hollow

An' tho' yon lowin heugh's†thy hame,
    Thou travels far;

backward

An' faith! thou's neither lag,† nor lame,

bashful;
afraid

    Nor blate,† nor scaur.†

4

Now

Whyles,† ranging like a roarin lion,
For prey, a' holes an' corners trying;
Whyles, on the strong-wing'd tempest flyin,

Stripping

    Tirlin†the kirks;
Whyles, in the human bosom pryin,
    Unseen thou lurks.

5

I've heard my rev'rend graunie say,
In lanely glens ye like to stray;
Or, where auld ruin'd castles grey
    Nod to the moon,
Ye fright the nightly wand'rer's way
    Wi' eldritch croon.

6

When twilight did my graunie summon,

sedate

To say her pray'rs, douce,† honest woman!

beyond

Aft yont†the dyke she's heard you bummin,
    Wi' eerie drone;

alders

Or, rustlin, thro' the boortrees†comin,
    Wi' heavy groan.

7

Ae dreary, windy, winter night,

squinting

The stars shot down wi' sklentin†light,
Wi' you mysel, I gat a fright:

pond

    Ayont the lough,†

clump of rushes

Ye, like a rash-buss,† stood in sight,

moan

    Wi' waving sugh.†

8

fist

The cudgel in my nieve†did shake,
Each bristl'd hair stood like a stake;

unearthly,
 harsh

When wi' an eldritch, stoor†'quaick, quaick,'
    Amang the springs,
Awa ye squatter'd like a drake,
    On whistling wings.

9

Let warlocks grim, an' wither'd hags,
Tell how wi' you, on ragweed nags,
They skim the muirs an' dizzy crags,
        Wi' wicked speed;
And in kirk-yards renew their leagues,
        Owre howkit† dead.   dug up

10

Thence, countra wives, wi' toil an' pain,
May plunge an' plunge the kirn† in vain;   churn
For O! the yellow treasure's taen
        By witching skill;
An' dawtit, twal-pint hawkie's gaen†   petted, twelve-pint cow's gone
        As yell's the bill.†   dry as the bull

11

Thence, mystic knots mak great abuse
On young guidmen,† fond, keen an' croose;†   husbands; confident or cocksure
When the best wark-lume† i' the house,   tool
        By cantraip† wit,   magic
Is instant made no worth a louse,
        Just at the bit.†   nick of time

12

When thowes dissolve the snawy hoord,†   hoard
An' float the jinglin icy boord,†   surface
Then, water-kelpies† haunt the foord,   sprites
        By your direction,
An' nighted trav'llers are allur'd
        To their destruction.

13

And aft your moss†-traversing spunkies†   bog; jack-o'-lanterns
Decoy the wight that late an' drunk is:
The bleezin,† curst, mischievous monkies†   blazing; will o' the wisps
        Delude his eyes,
Till in some miry slough he sunk is,
        Ne'er mair to rise.

14

When Masons' mystic word an' grip
In storms an' tempests raise you up,
Some cock or cat your rage maun† stop,   must
        Or, strange to tell!
The youngest brother ye wad whip
        Aff straught† to hell.   straight

15

garden

Lang syne in Eden's bonie yard,†
When youthfu' lovers first were pair'd,
An' all the soul of love they shar'd,
          The raptur'd hour,
Sweet on the fragrant flow'ry swaird,
          In shady bow'r:

16

scheming

Then you, ye auld, snick-drawing†dog!
Ye cam to Paradise incog,

trick

An' play'd on man a cursed brogue†
          (Black be your fa'!),

shake

An' gied the infant warld a shog,†
          'Maist ruin'd a'.

17

flurry

D'ye mind that day when in a bizz†

smoky; scorched wig

Wi' reekit†duds, an' reestit gizz,†

smutty

Ye did present your smoutie†phiz
          'Mang better folk;

squinted

An' sklented†on the man of Uzz
          Your spitefu' joke?

18

An' how ye gat him i' your thrall,
An' brak him out o' house an' hal',
While scabs an' botches did him gall,
          Wi' bitter claw;

loosed; scold

An' lows'd†his ill-tongu'd wicked scaul†–

of all

          Was warst ava?†

19

But a' your doings to rehearse,

fighting

Your wily snares an' fechtin†fierce,
Sin' that day Michael did you pierce
          Down to this time,

beat; Lowland

Wad ding†a Lallan†tongue, or Erse,
          In prose or rhyme.

20

Hoofs

An' now, Auld Cloots,† I ken ye're thinkin,

roistering

A certain Bardie's rantin,† drinkin,

hurrying

Some luckless hour will send him linkin,†
          To your black Pit;

dodging

But, faith! he'll turn a corner jinkin,†
          An' cheat you yet.

But fare-you-weel, Auld Nickie-Ben!
O, wad ye tak a thought an' men'!
Ye aiblins[†]might – I dinna ken –   perhaps
        Still hae a stake:
I'm wae[†]to think upo' yon den,   sad
        Ev'n for your sake!

THE
DEATH AND DYING WORDS OF
POOR MAILIE[†]   Mollie

THE AUTHOR'S ONLY PET YOWE:[†]   ewe
AN UNCO[†] MOURNFU' TALE   very

As Mailie, an' her lambs thegither,[†]   together
Was ae[†]day nibblin on the tether,   one
Upon her cloot[†]she coost a hitch,[†]   hoof; looped
An' owre she warsl'd[†]in the ditch: floundered
There, groanin, dying, she did lie,
When Hughoc he cam doytin[†]by.   doddering

    Wi' glowrin[†]een,[†] an' lifted han's   staring; eyes
Poor Hughoc like a statue stan's;
He saw her days were near-hand[†] ended,   almost
But, wae's[†]my heart! he could na mend it!   woe
He gapèd wide, but naething spak.
At length poor Mailie silence brak: –

    'O thou, whase lamentable face
Appears to mourn my woefu' case!
My dying words attentive hear,
An' bear them to my Master dear.

own   'Tell him, if e'er again he keep[†]

much money   As muckle gear[†]as buy a sheep –
               O, bid him never tie them mair,
               Wi' wicked strings o' hemp or hair!

drive   But ca'[†]them out to park or hill,
               An' let them wander at their will:
               So may his flock increase, an' grow
               To scores o' lambs, an' packs o' woo'!

               'Tell him, he was a Master kin',
               An' ay was guid to me an' mine;
               An' now my dying charge I gie him,
               My helpless lambs, I trust them wi' him.

               'O bid him save their harmless lives,

foxes   Frae dogs, an' tods,[†] an' butchers' knives!
               But gie them guid cow-milk their fill,

look after   Till they be fit to fend[†]themsel;

tend   An' tent[†]them duly, e'en an' morn,

small quantities; Wi' teats[†]o' hay an' ripps[†]o' corn.
  handfuls

ways   'An' may they never learn the gaets,[†]

restless   Of ither vile, wanrestfu'[†]pets –

gaps   To slink thro' slaps,[†] an' reave an' steal,

cabbage stalks At stacks o' pease, or stocks o' kail![†]
               So may they, like their great forbears,
               For monie a year come thro' the sheers:
               So wives will gie them bits o' bread,

weep   An' bairns greet[†]for them when they're dead.

ram   'My poor toop[†]-lamb, my son an' heir,
               O, bid him breed him up wi' care!
               An' if he live to be a beast,

conduct   To pit some havins[†]in his breast!

will not   An' warn him – what I winna[†]name –

ewes   To stay content wi' yowes[†]at hame;
               An' no to rin an' wear his cloots,

unmannerly   Like other menseless,[†] graceless brutes.

next; ewekin;   'An' niest,[†] my yowie,[†] silly[†]thing;
  helpless   Gude keep thee frae a tether string!

make friends   O, may thou ne'er forgather[†]up,
               Wi' onie blastit, moorland toop;

nibble; meddle But ay keep mind to moop[†]an' mell,[†]
               Wi' sheep o' credit like thysel!

'And now, my bairns, wi' my last breath,
I lea'e my blessin wi' you baith:
An' when you think upo' your mither,
Mind to be kind to ane anither.

'Now, honest Hughoc, dinna fail,
To tell my master a' my tale;
An' bid him burn this cursed tether,
An' for thy pains thou'se get my blether.'† bladder

This said, poor Mailie turn'd her head,
An' clos'd her een†amang the dead! eyes

POOR MAILIE'S ELEGY

1

Lament in rhyme, lament in prose,
Wi' saut tears tricklin down your nose;
Our Bardie's fate is at a close,
   Past a' remead!† remedy
The last, sad cape-stane of his woes;
   Poor Mailie's dead!

2

It's no the loss of warl's gear,† worldly pelf
That could sae bitter draw the tear,
Or mak our Bardie, dowie,† wear drooping
   The mourning weed:
He's lost a friend an' neebor dear
   In Mailie dead.

3

Thro' a' the toun†she trotted by him; farm
A lang half-mile she could descry him;
Wi' kindly bleat, when she did spy him,
   She ran wi' speed:
A friend mair faithfu' ne'er cam nigh him,
   Than Mailie dead.

4

I wat†she was a sheep o' sense, knew
An' could behave hersel wi' mense:† tact
I'll say't, she never brak a fence,
   Thro' thievish greed.
Our Bardie, lanely, keeps the spence† parlor
   Sin' Mailie's dead.

[25]

5

glen

Or, if he wanders up the howe,[†]
Her livin image in her yowe

knoll

Comes bleatin till him, owre the knowe,[†]
For bits o' bread;

roll

An' down the briny pearls rowe[†]
For Mailie dead.

6

issue; rams

She was nae get[†]o' moorlan tips,[†]

matted fleece; rumps

Wi' tawted ket,[†] an' hairy hips;[†]
For her forbears were brought in ships,
Frae 'yont the Tweed:

fleece; shears

A bonier fleesh[†]ne'er cross'd the clips[†]
Than Mailie's dead.

7

Woe befall

Wae worth[†]the man wha first did shape

dangerous; rope

That vile, wanchancie[†] thing – a rape![†]

grit teeth

It maks guid fellows girn[†]an' gape,
Wi' chokin dread;
An' Robin's bonnet wave wi' crape
For Mailie dead.

8

O a' ye bards on bonie Doon!

bagpipes

An' wha on Ayr your chanters[†]tune!
Come, join the melancholious croon
O' Robin's reed!

rejoice

His heart will never get aboon![†]
His Mailie's dead!

EPISTLE TO JAMES SMITH

Friendship, mysterious cement of the soul!
Sweet'ner of Life, and solder of Society!
I owe thee much —

BLAIR

1

Dear Smith, the slee'st, pawkie†thief,   artful
That e'er attempted stealth or rief!†   plunder
Ye surely hae some warlock-breef†   wizard-spell
             Owre human hearts;
For ne'er a bosom yet was prief†   proof
             Against your arts.

2

For me, I swear by sun an' moon,
And ev'ry star that blinks aboon,†   above
Ye've cost me twenty pair o' shoon,
             Just gaun†to see you;   going
And ev'ry ither pair that's done,
             Mair taen†I'm wi' you.   taken

3

That auld, capricious carlin,† Nature,   gossip
To mak amends for scrimpit†stature,   stunted
She's turn'd you off, a human-creature
             On her first plan;
And in her freaks, on ev'ry feature
             She's wrote the Man.

4

Just now I've taen the fit o' rhyme,
My barmie noddle's†working prime,   seething brain
My fancy yerkit†up sublime,   stirred
             Wi' hasty summon:
Hae ye a leisure-moment's time
             To hear what's comin?

5

Some rhyme a neebor's name to lash;
Some rhyme (vain thought!) for needfu' cash;
Some rhyme to court the countra clash,†   talk
             An' raise a din;
For me, an aim I never fash;†   trouble about
             I rhyme for fun.

6

The star that rules my luckless lot,
Has fated me the russet coat,
fourpence   An' damn'd my fortune to the groat;[†]
       But, in requit,
Has blest me with a random-shot
       O' countra wit.

7

turn   This while my notion's taen a sklent,[†]
To try my fate in guid, black prent;
But still the mair I'm that way bent,
Softly!   Something cries, 'Hoolie![†]
advise; heed   I red[†]you, honest man, tak tent![†]
       Ye'll shaw your folly:

8

'There's ither poets, much your betters,
Far seen in Greek, deep men o' letters,
Hae thought they had ensur'd their debtors,
       A' future ages;
Now moths deform, in shapeless tatters,
       Their unknown pages.'

9

Then farewell hopes o' laurel-boughs
To garland my poetic brows!
Henceforth I'll rove where busy ploughs
at work   Are whistling thrang;[†]
hollows   An' teach the lanely heights an' howes[†]
       My rustic sang.

10

careless   I'll wander on, wi' tentless[†]heed
How never-halting moments speed,
Till Fate shall snap the brittle thread;
       Then, all unknown,
I'll lay me with th' inglorious dead,
       Forgot and gone!

11

But why o' death begin a tale?
well   Just now we're living sound an' hale;[†]
Then top and maintop crowd the sail,
       Heave Care o'er-side!
And large, before Enjoyment's gale,
       Let's tak the tide.

12

This life, sae far's I understand,
Is a' enchanted fairy-land,
Where Pleasure is the magic-wand,
   That, wielded right,
Maks hours like minutes, hand in hand,
   Dance by fu' light.

13

The magic-wand then let us wield;
For, ance that five-an'-forty's speel'd,[†]   passed
See, crazy, weary, joyless Eild,[†]   Eld
   Wi' wrinkl'd face,
Comes hostin,[†] hirplin[†] owre the field,   coughing;
   Wi' creepin pace.   limping

14

When ance life's day draws near the gloamin,[†]   twilight
Then fareweel vacant, careless roamin;
An' fareweel chearfu' tankards foamin,
   An' social noise:
An' fareweel dear, deluding Woman,
   The joy of joys!

15

O Life! how pleasant, in thy morning,
Young Fancy's rays the hills adorning!
Cold-pausing Caution's lesson scorning,
   We frisk away,
Like school-boys, at th' expected warning,
   To joy an' play.

16

We wander there, we wander here,
We eye the rose upon the brier,
Unmindful that the thorn is near,
   Among the leaves;
And tho' the puny wound appear,
   Short while it grieves.

17

Some, lucky, find a flow'ry spot,
For which they never toil'd nor swat;[†]   sweated
They drink the sweet and eat the fat,
   But[†] care or pain;   Without
And haply eye the barren hut
   With high disdain.

[29]

18

With steady aim, some Fortune chase;
Keen Hope does ev'ry sinew brace;
Thro' fair, thro' foul, they urge the race,
      And seize the prey:

quiet; snug Then cannie,[†] in some cozie[†]place,
      They close the day.

19

And others, like your humble servan',
Poor wights! nae rules nor roads observin,
To right or left eternal swervin,
      They zig-zag on;
Till, curst with age, obscure an' starvin,
      They aften groan.

20

Alas! what bitter toil an' straining –
But truce with peevish, poor complaining!
Is Fortune's fickle *Luna* waning?
      E'en let her gang!
Beneath what light she has remaining,
      Let's sing our sang.

21

My pen I here fling to the door,
And kneel, ye Pow'rs! and warm implore,
'Tho' I should wander *Terra* o'er,
      In all her climes,
Grant me but this, I ask no more,
plenty   Ay rowth[†]o' rhymes.

22

dripping 'Gie dreeping[†]roasts to countra lairds,
Till icicles hing frae their beards;
clothes Gie fine braw claes[†]to fine life-guards
      And maids of honor;
ale; tinkers And yill[†]an' whisky gie to cairds,[†]
sicken   Until they sconner.[†]

23

'A title, Dempster merits it;
A garter gie to Willie Pitt;
Gie wealth to some be-ledger'd cit,
      In cent. per cent.;
But give me real, sterling wit,
      And I'm content.

24

'While ye are pleas'd to keep me hale,
I'll sit down o'er my scanty meal,
Be't water-brose[†]or muslin-kail,[†]
        Wi' cheerfu' face,
As lang's the Muses dinna fail
        To say the grace.'

meal and water; beefless broth

25

An anxious e'e I never throws
Behint my lug,[†] or by my nose;
I jouk[†]beneath Misfortune's blows
        As weel's I may;
Sworn foe to sorrow, care, and prose,
        I rhyme away.

ear
duck

26

O ye douce[†]folk that live by rule,
Grave, tideless-blooded, calm an' cool,
Compar'd wi' you – O fool! fool! fool!
        How much unlike!
Your hearts are just a standing pool,
        Your lives a dyke![†]

sedate

ditch

27

Nae hair-brained, sentimental traces
In your unletter'd, nameless faces!
In *arioso* trills and graces
        Ye never stray;
But *gravissimo*, solemn basses
        Ye hum away.

28

Ye are sae grave, nae doubt ye're wise;
Nae ferly[†]tho' ye do despise
The hairum-scairum, ram-stam[†]boys,
        The rattling squad:
I see ye upward cast your eyes –
        Ye ken the road!

marvel
headlong

29

Whilst I – but I shall haud[†]me there,
Wi' you I'll scarce gang onie where –
Then, Jamie, I shall say nae mair,
        But quat[†]my sang,
Content wi' you to mak a pair,
        Whare'er I gang.

hold

quit

THE AULD FARMER'S
NEW-YEAR MORNING SALUTATION
TO HIS AULD MARE, MAGGIE

ON GIVING HER THE ACCUSTOMED RIPP OF
CORN TO HANSEL IN THE NEW-YEAR

1

handful from   A Guid New-Year I wish thee, Maggie!
the sheaf; belly   Hae, there's a ripp[†]to thy auld baggie:[†]
hollow-backed;   Tho' thou's howe-backit[†]now, an' knaggie,[†]
  knobby   I've seen the day
gone; stag   Thou could hae gaen[†]like onie staggie,[†]
lea   Out-owre the lay.[†]

2

drooping   Tho' now thou's dowie,[†] stiff, an' crazy,
        An' thy auld hide as white's a daisie,
shiny   I've seen thee dappl't,[†] sleek an' glaizie,
              A bonie gray:
prepared;   He should been tight that daur't[†]to raize[†]thee,
  excite   Ance in a day.

3

        Thou ance was i' the foremost rank,
stately; compact;   A filly buirdly,[†] steeve,[†] an' swank;[†]
  limber   An' set weel down a shapely shank
earth   As e'er tread yird;[†]
swampy spot   An' could hae flown out-owre a stank[†]
              Like onie bird.

4

It's now some nine-an'-twenty year
Sin' thou was my guid-father's†meere; — father-in-law's
He gied me thee, o' tocher clear,† — wholly as dowry
        An' fifty mark;
Tho' it was sma', 'twas weel-won gear,
        An' thou was stark.† — strong

5

When first I gaed†to woo my Jenny, — went
Ye then was trottin wi' your minnie:† — mother
Tho' ye was trickie, slee,† an' funnie, — sly
        Ye ne'er was donsie;† — vicious
But hamely, tawie,† quiet, an' cannie, — tractable
        An' unco sonsie.† — good-tempered

6

That day, ye pranc'd wi' muckle pride,
When ye bure hame my bonie bride:
An' sweet an' gracefu' she did ride,
        Wi' maiden air!
Kyle-Stewart I could bragged wide,† — have challenged
        For sic a pair.

7

Tho' now ye dow†but hoyte†and hobble, — can; limp
An' wintle†like a saumont-coble,† — stagger; salmon-boat
That day, ye was a jinker†noble, — goer
        For heels an' win'!† — wind
An' ran them till they a' did wauble,† — wobble
        Far, far behin'!

8

When thou an' I were young and skiegh,† — skittish
An' stable-meals at fairs were driegh,† — tedious
How thou wad prance, an' snore,† an' skriegh,† — snort; whinny
        An' tak the road!
Town's-bodies ran, an' stood abiegh,† — aloof
        An' ca't thee mad.

9

When thou was corn't,† an' I was mellow, — had oats
We took the road ay like a swallow:
At brooses†thou had ne'er a fellow, — wedding-races
        For pith an' speed;
But ev'ry tail thou pay't them hollow,
        Whare'er thou gaed.

10

short-rumped — The sma', droop-rumpl't,† hunter cattle,
have beat; spurt — Might aiblins waur't†thee for a brattle;†
But sax Scotch miles thou try't their mettle,
wheeze — An' gar't them whaizle:†
switch — Nae whip nor spur, but just a wattle†
willow — O' saugh†or hazle.

11

plough-horse — Thou was a noble fittie-lan',†
As e'er in tug or tow was drawn!
eight; past — Aft thee an' I, in aught†hours' gaun,†
On guid March-weather,
1½ acres — Hae turn'd sax rood†beside our han'
For days thegither.

12

pulled rashly;
stopped suddenly;
capered — Thou never braing't,† an' fetch't,† an' fliskit;†
But thy auld tail thou wad hae whiskit,
An' spread abreed thy weel-fill'd brisket,
rooty hillocks would
have reared;
cracked — Wi' pith an' pow'r;
Till sprittie knowes wad rair't,† an' riskit,†
fallen smoothly over — An' slypet owre.†

13

When frosts lay lang, an' snaws were deep,
An' threaten'd labour back to keep,
dish — I gied thy cog†a wee bit heap
edge — Aboon the timmer:†
I ken'd my Maggie wad na sleep
Ere — For†that, or simmer.

14

balked — In cart or car thou never reestit;†
stiffest incline — The steyest brae†thou wad hae fac't it;
leaped; sprang — Thou never lap,† an' sten't,† an' breastit,
Then stood to blaw;
But just thy step a wee thing hastit,
jogged along — Thou snoov't awa.†

15

team; issue — My pleugh†is now thy bairntime†a',
Four gallant brutes as e'er did draw;
Besides six
more — Forbye sax mae†I've sell't awa,
That thou hast nurst:
They drew me thretteen pund an' twa,
The vera warst.

16

Monie a sair darg† we twa hae wrought,   day's work
An' wi' the weary warl' fought!
An' monie an anxious day I thought
            We wad be beat!
Yet here to crazy age we're brought,
            Wi' something yet.

17

An' think na, my auld trusty servan',
That now perhaps thou's less deservin,
An' thy auld days may end in starvin;
            For my last fow,†   bushel
A heapet stimpart,† I'll reserve ane   quarter-peck
            Laid by for you.

18

We've worn to crazy years thegither;
We'll toyte† about wi' ane anither;   totter
Wi' tentie care I'll flit† thy tether   change
            To some hain'd rig,†   reserved patch
Whare ye may nobly rax your leather†   fill your stomach
            Wi' sma' fatigue.

TO A MOUSE

ON TURNING HER UP IN HER NEST
WITH THE PLOUGH,
NOVEMBER 1785

1

Wee, sleekit,† cowrin, tim'rous beastie,   sleek
O, what a panic's in thy breastie!
Thou need na start awa sae hasty
            Wi' bickering brattle!†   hurrying scamper
I wad be laith† to rin an' chase thee,   loath
            Wi' murdering pattle!†   plough-staff

2

I'm truly sorry man's dominion
Has broken Nature's social union,
An' justifies that ill opinion
            Which makes thee startle
At me, thy poor, earth-born companion
            An' fellow mortal!

3

sometimes

I doubt na, whyles,[†] but thou may thieve;
What then? poor beastie, thou maun live!

odd ear;
  sheaf

A daimen icker[†]in a thrave[†]
                'S a sma' request;

what's left

I'll get a blessin wi' the lave,[†]
                An' never miss't!

4

Thy wee-bit housie, too, in ruin!

feeble walls; winds

Its silly wa's[†]the win's[†]are strewin!

build

An' naething, now, to big[†]a new ane,

coarse grass

                O' foggage green![†]
An' bleak December's win's ensuin,

bitter

                Baith snell[†]an' keen!

5

Thou saw the fields laid bare an' waste,
An' weary winter comin fast,
An' cozie here, beneath the blast,
                Thou thought to dwell,
Till crash! the cruel coulter past
                Out thro' thy cell.

6

stubble

That wee bit heap o' leaves an' stibble,[†]
Has cost thee monie a weary nibble!
Now thou's turned out, for a' thy trouble,

Without; holding

                But[†]house or hald,[†]

endure

To thole[†]the winter's sleety dribble,

hoar-frost

                An' cranreuch[†]cauld!

[36]

7

But Mousie, thou art no thy lane,†
In proving foresight may be vain:
The best-laid schemes o' mice an' men
        Gang aft agley,†
An' lea'e us nought but grief an' pain,
        For promis'd joy!

alone

askew

8

Still thou art blest, compared wi' me!
The present only toucheth thee:
But och! I backward cast my e'e,
        On prospects drear!
An' forward, tho' I canna see,
        I guess an' fear!

EPISTLE TO
DAVIE, A BROTHER POET

JANUARY

1

While winds frae aff Ben-Lomond blaw,
And bar the doors wi' drivin' snaw,
   And hing us owre the ingle,†
I set me down to pass the time,
And spin a verse or twa o' rhyme,
   In hamely, westlin†jingle:
While frosty winds blaw in the drift,
   Ben to the chimla lug,†
I grudge a wee the great-folk's gift,
    That live sae bien†an' snug:
      I tent†less, and want less
        Their roomy fire-side;
      But hanker, and canker,
        To see their cursed pride.

fire

westland

*Right to the
chimney corner*

prosperous
value

2

It's hardly in a body's pow'r,
To keep, at times, frae being sour,
   To see how things are shar'd;
How best o' chiels†are whyles†in want,
While coofs†on countless thousands rant,†
   And ken na how to ware't;†

chaps; sometimes
dolts; roister
spend

trouble
wealth

ask not
fig

whole; sound

But Davie, lad, ne'er fash†your head,
    Tho' we hae little gear;†
We're fit to win our daily bread,
    As lang's we're hale†and fier:†
      'Mair spier na,† nor fear na,'
        Auld age ne'er mind a feg;†
        The last o't, the warst o't,
        Is only but to beg.

3

To lie in kilns and barns at e'en,
When banes are craz'd, and bluid is thin,
    Is, doubtless, great distress!
Yet then content could make us blest;
Ev'n then, sometimes, we'd snatch a taste
    Of truest happiness.
The honest heart that's free frae a'
    Intended fraud or guile,
However Fortune kick the ba',
    Has ay some cause to smile;
      And mind still, you'll find still,
        A comfort this nae sma';
      Nae mair then, we'll care then,
        Nae farther can we fa'.

4

Without;
  holding

hill-sides
hum
Then

What tho', like commoners of air,
We wander out, we know not where,
    But†either house or hal'?†
Yet Nature's charms, the hills and woods,
The sweeping vales, and foaming floods,
    Are free alike to all.
In days when daisies deck the ground,
    And blackbirds whistle clear,
With honest joy our hearts will bound,
    To see the coming year:
      On braes†when we please then,
        We'll sit an' sowth†a tune;
      Syne†rhyme till't we'll time till't,
        An' sing't when we hae done.

5

It's no in titles nor in rank:
It's no in wealth like Lon'on Bank,

To purchase peace and rest.
It's no in makin muckle, mair;[†]   much, more
It's no in books, it's no in lear,[†]   learning
  To make us truly blest:
If happiness hae not her seat
  An' centre in the breast,
We may be wise, or rich, or great,
  But never can be blest!
    Nae treasures nor pleasures
      Could make us happy lang;
    The heart ay's the part ay
      That makes us right or wrang.

6

Think ye, that sic as you and I,
Wha drudge and drive thro' wet and dry,
  Wi' never ceasing toil;
Think ye, are we less blest than they,
Wha scarcely tent[†] us in their way,   notice
  As hardly worth their while?
Alas! how oft, in haughty mood,
  God's creatures they oppress!
Or else, neglecting a' that's guid,
  They riot in excess!
    Baith careless and fearless
      Of either Heaven or Hell;
    Esteeming and deeming
      It a' an idle tale!

7

Then let us chearfu' acquiesce,
Nor make our scanty pleasures less
  By pining at our state:
And, even should misfortunes come,
I here wha sit hae met wi' some,
  An's[†] thankfu' for them yet,   And am
They gie the wit of age to youth;
  They let us ken oursel;
They make us see the naked truth,
  The real guid and ill:
    Tho' losses and crosses
      Be lessons right severe,
    There's wit there, ye'll get there,
      Ye'll find nae other where.

8

listen to   But tent†me, Davie, ace o' hearts!
cards   (To say aught less wad wrang the cartes,†
                And flatt'ry I detest)
This life has joys for you and I;
And joys that riches ne'er could buy,
    And joys the very best.
There's a' the pleasures o' the heart,
    The lover an' the frien':
Ye hae your Meg, your dearest part,
    And I my darling Jean!
        It warms me, it charms me
            To mention but her name:
kindles   It heats me, it beets†me,
            And sets me a' on flame!

9

O all ye Pow'rs who rule above!
O Thou whose very self art love!
    Thou know'st my words sincere!
The life-blood streaming thro' my heart,
Or my more dear immortal part,
    Is not more fondly dear!
When heart-corroding care and grief
    Deprive my soul of rest,
Her dear idea brings relief
    And solace to my breast.
        Thou Being All-seeing,
           O, hear my fervent pray'r!
        Still take her, and make her
           Thy most peculiar care!

10

All hail! ye tender feelings dear!
The smile of love, the friendly tear,
    The sympathetic glow!
Long since, this world's thorny ways
Had number'd out my weary days,
    Had it not been for you!
Fate still has blest me with a friend
    In every care and ill;
And oft a more endearing band,
    A tie more tender still.
        It lightens, it brightens
           The tenebrific scene,

To meet with, and greet with
My Davie or my Jean!

11

O, how that Name inspires my style!
The words come skelpin'†rank an' file,   skipping
Amaist†before I ken!   almost
The ready measure rins as fine,
As Phoebus and the famous Nine
Were glowrin owre†my pen.   overlooking
My spaviet†Pegasus will limp,   spavined
Till ance he's fairly het;†   hot
And then he'll hilch,† an' stilt,† an' jimp,†   hobble; limp; jump
And rin an unco fit;†   uncommon burst
But least then, the beast then
Should rue this hasty ride,
I'll light now, and dight†now   wipe
His sweaty, wizen'd hide.

TO A MOUNTAIN DAISY

1

Wee, modest, crimson-tippèd flow'r,
Thou's met me in an evil hour;
For I maun crush amang the stoure†   dust
Thy slender stem:
To spare thee now is past my pow'r,
Thou bonie gem.

2

Alas! it's no thy neebor sweet,
The bonie lark, companion meet,
Bending thee 'mang the dewy weet,†   wet
Wi' spreckl'd breast!
When upward-springing, blythe, to greet
The purpling east.

3

Cauld blew the bitter-biting north
Upon thy early, humble birth;

sparkled Yet cheerfully thou glinted†forth
　　　　Amid the storm,
Scarce rear'd above the parent-earth
　　　　Thy tender form.

4

The flaunting flow'rs our gardens yield,

walls; must High shelt'ring woods and wa's†maun†shield;

shelter But thou, beneath the random bield†
　　　　O' clod or stane,

bare stubble- Adorns the histie stibble-field,†
field 　　　　Unseen, alane.

5

There, in thy scanty mantle clad,
Thy snawie bosom sun-ward spread,
Thou lifts thy unassuming head
　　　　In humble guise;
But now the share uptears thy bed,
　　　　And low thou lies!

6

Such is the fate of artless maid,
Sweet flow'ret of the rural shade!
By love's simplicity betray'd,
　　　　And guileless trust;
Till she, like thee, all soil'd, is laid
　　　　Low i' the dust.

7

Such is the fate of simple Bard,
On Life's rough ocean luckless starr'd!
Unskilful he to note the card
　　　　Of prudent lore,
Till billows rage, and gales blow hard,
　　　　And whelm him o'er!

8

Such fate to suffering Worth is giv'n,
Who long with wants and woes has striv'n,
By human pride or cunning driv'n
　　　　To mis'ry's brink;
Till, wrench'd of ev'ry stay but Heav'n,
　　　　He, ruin'd, sink!

Ev'n thou who mourn'st the Daisy's fate,
That fate is thine – no distant date;
Stern Ruin's plough-share drives elate,
      Full on thy bloom,
Till crush'd beneath the furrow's weight
      Shall be thy doom!

EPISTLE TO
A YOUNG FRIEND

MAY — 1786

1

I lang hae thought, my youthfu' friend,
  A something to have sent you,
Tho' it should serve nae ither end
  Than just a kind memento:
But how the subject-theme may gang,
  Let time and chance determine:
Perhaps it may turn out a sang;
  Perhaps, turn out a sermon.

2

Ye'll try the world soon, my lad;
  And, Andrew dear, believe me,
Ye'll find mankind an unco⁺squad,   strange
  And muckle they may grieve ye:
For care and trouble set your thought,
  Ev'n when your end's attainéd;
And a' your views may come to nought,
  Where ev'ry nerve is strainéd.

3

I'll no say, men are villains a':
  The real, harden'd wicked,
Wha hae nae check but human law,
  Are to a few restricked;
But, och! mankind are unco⁺weak   mighty
  An' little to be trusted;
If Self the wavering balance shake,
  It's rarely right adjusted!

4

Yet they wha fa' in Fortune's strife,
    Their fate we should na censure;
For still, th' important end of life
    They equally may answer:
A man may hae an honest heart,
poverty   Tho' poortith⁺hourly stare him;
A man may tak a neebor's part,
    Yet hae nae cash to spare him.

5

Ay free, aff han', your story tell,
    When wi' a bosom cronie;
But still keep something to yoursel
    Ye scarcely tell to onie:
Conceal yoursel as weel's ye can
    Frae critical dissection:
pry   But keek⁺thro' ev'ry other man
    Wi' sharpen'd, sly inspection.

6

flame   The sacred lowe⁺o' weel-plac'd love,
    Luxuriantly indulge it;
attempt   But never tempt⁺th' illicit rove,
    Tho' naething should divulge it:
I waive the quantum o' the sin,
    The hazard of concealing;
But, och! it hardens a' within,
    And petrifies the feeling!

7

To catch Dame Fortune's golden smile,
    Assiduous wait upon her;
And gather gear by ev'ry wile
    That's justify'd by honor:
Not for to hide it in a hedge,
    Nor for a train-attendant;
But for the glorious privilege
    Of being independent.

8

The fear o' Hell's a hangman's whip
    To haud the wretch in order;
But where ye feel your honor grip,
    Let that ay be your border:

Its slightest touches, instant pause –
    Debar a' side-pretences;
And resolutely keep its laws,
    Uncaring consequences.

9

The great Creator to revere
    Must sure become the creature;
But still the preaching cant forbear,
    And ev'n the rigid feature:
Yet ne'er with wits profane to range
    Be complaisance extended;
An atheist-laugh's a poor exchange
    For Deity offended!

10

When ranting'round in Pleasure's ring,   frolicking
    Religion may be blinded;
Or if she gie a random sting,
    It may be little minded;
But when on Life we're tempest-driv'n –
    A conscience but a canker –
A correspondence fix'd wi' Heav'n
    Is sure a noble anchor!

11

Adieu, dear, amiable youth!
    Your heart can ne'er be wanting!
May prudence, fortitude, and truth,
    Erect your brow undaunting!
In ploughman phrase, 'God send you speed,'
    Still daily to grow wiser;
And may ye better reck the rede,†   heed the
    Than ever did th' adviser!   counsel

ON A SCOTCH BARD

GONE TO THE WEST INDIES

1

sips   A' ye wha live by sowps†o' drink,
rhyme   A' ye wha live by crambo-clink,†
              A' ye wha live and never think,
                    Come, mourn wi' me!
comrade;   Our billie's†gien us a' a jink,†
  given us all
   the slip   An' owre the sea!

2

jovial set   Lament him a' ye rantin core,†
frolic   Wha dearly like a random-splore;†
              Nae mair he'll join the merry roar
                    In social key;
              For now he's taen anither shore,
                    An' owre the sea!

3

wish   The bonie lasses weel may wiss†him,
              And in their dear petitions place him:
              The widows, wives, an' a' may bless him
                    Wi' tearfu' e'e,
wot   For weel I wat†they'll sairly miss him
                    That's owre the sea!

4

             O Fortune, they hae room to grumble!
drone   Hadst thou taen aff some drowsy bummle,†
fuss   Wha can do nought but fyke†an' fumble,
                  'Twad been nae plea;
nimble;   But he was gleg†as onie wumble,†
  wimble   That's owre the sea!

5

cheerful   Auld, cantie†Kyle may weepers wear,
             An' stain them wi' the saut, saut tear:
             'Twill mak her poor auld heart, I fear,
                    In flinders flee:
             He was her Laureat monie a year,
                    That's owre the sea!

6

             He saw Misfortune's cauld nor-west
             Lang-mustering up a bitter blast;

A jillet[†]brak his heart at last,
      Ill may she be!
So, took a birth[†]afore the mast,
      An' owre the sea.

jilt

berth

7

To tremble under Fortune's cummock,[†]
On scarce a bellyfu' o' drummock,[†]
Wi' his proud, independent stomach,
      Could ill agree;
So, row't[†]his hurdies[†]in a hammock,
      An' owre the sea.

rod

*meal and
'water*

*rolled;
buttocks*

8

He ne'er was gien to great misguiding,[†]
Yet coin his pouches[†]wad na bide in;
Wi' him it ne'er was under hiding,
      He dealt it free:
The Muse was a' that he took pride in,
      That's owre the sea.

transgression

pockets

9

Jamaica bodies, use him weel,
An' hap[†]him in a cozie biel:[†]
Ye'll find him ay a dainty chiel,[†]
      An' fou o' glee:
He wad na[†]wrang'd the vera Deil,
      That's owre the sea.

shelter; place

fellow

*would not
have*

10

Fareweel, my rhyme-composing billie!
Your native soil was right ill-willie;[†]
But may ye flourish like a lily,
      Now bonilie!
I'll toast you in my hindmost gillie,[†]
      Tho' owre the sea!

unkind

last gill

A DEDICATION

TO GAVIN HAMILTON, ESQ.

wheedling,
flattering

praise

Expect na, Sir, in this narration,
A fleechin, fleth'rin[†]Dedication,
To roose[†]you up, an' ca' you guid,
An' sprung o' great an' noble bluid,
Because ye're surnam'd like His Grace,
Perhaps related to the race:
Then, when I'm tired – and sae are ye,
Wi' monie a fulsome, sinfu' lie –
Set up a face how I stop short,
For fear your modesty be hurt.

bellyful

low

cannot; nag

This may do – maun do, Sir, wi' them wha
Maun please the great-folk for a wamefou';[†]
For me! sae laigh[†]I need na bow,
For, Lord be thankit, I can plough;
And when I downa[†]yoke a naig,[†]
Then, Lord be thankit, I can beg;
Sae I shall say, an' that's nae flatt'rin,
It's just sic poet an' sic patron.

trounce

The Poet, some guid angel help him,
Or else, I fear, some ill ane skelp[†]him!
He may do weel for a' he's done yet,
But only he's no just begun yet.

The Patron (sir, ye maun forgie me;
I winna lie, come what will o' me),
On ev'ry hand it will allow'd be,
He's just – nae better than he should be.

sometimes

I readily and freely grant,
He downa see a poor man want;
What's no his ain he winna tak it;
What ance he says, he winna break it;
Ought he can lend he'll no refus't,
Till aft his guidness is abus'd;
And rascals whyles[†]that do him wrang,
Ev'n that, he does na mind it lang;
As master, landlord, husband, father,
He does na fail his part in either.

But then, nae thanks to him for a' that;
Nae godly symptom ye can ca' that;
It's naething but a milder feature
Of our poor, sinfu', corrupt nature:
Ye'll get the best o' moral works,
'Mang black Gentoos,† and pagan Turks,   Hindus
Or hunters wild on Ponotaxi,
Wha never heard of orthodoxy.
That he's the poor man's friend in need,
The gentleman in word and deed,
It's no thro' terror of damnation:
It's just a carnal inclination,
And och! that's nae regeneration.

Morality, thou deadly bane,
Thy tens o' thousands thou hast slain!
Vain is his hope, whase stay an' trust is
In moral mercy, truth, and justice!

No – stretch a point to catch a plack;†   farthing
Abuse a brother to his back;
Steal thro' the winnock†frae a whore,   window
But point the rake that taks the door;
Be to the poor like onie whunstane,†   granite
And haud their noses to the grunstane;†   grindstone
Ply ev'ry art o' legal thieving;
No matter – stick to sound believing.

Learn three-mile pray'rs, an' half-mile graces,
Wi' weel-spread looves,† an' lang, wry faces;   palms
Grunt up a solemn, lengthen'd groan,
And damn a' parties but your own;
I'll warrant then, ye're nae deceiver,
A steady, sturdy, staunch believer.

O ye wha leave the springs o' Calvin,
For gumlie dubs†of your ain delvin!   muddy
Ye sons of Heresy and Error,   puddles
Ye'll some day squeel in quaking terror,
When Vengeance draws the sword in wrath,
And in the fire throws the sheath;
When Ruin, with his sweeping besom,
Just frets till Heav'n commission gies him;
While o'er the harp pale Misery moans,
And strikes the ever-deep'ning tones,
Still louder shrieks, and heavier groans!

Your pardon, sir, for this digression:
I maist[†]forgat my Dedication; *(almost)*
But when divinity comes 'cross me,
My readers still are sure to lose me.

So, Sir, you see 'twas nae daft[†]vapor; *(mad)*
But I maturely thought it proper,
When a' my works I did review,
To dedicate them, Sir, to you:
Because (ye need na tak' it ill),
I thought them something like yoursel.

Then patronize them wi' your favor
And your petitioner shall ever —
I had amaist said, ever pray,
But that's a word I need na say;
For prayin, I hae little skill o't, *(extremely reluctant; bad at it)*
I'm baith dead-sweer,[†] an' wretched ill o't;[†]
But I'se[†]repeat each poor man's pray'r, *(I'll)*
That kens or hears about you, Sir: —

'May ne'er Misfortune's gowling[†]bark *(howling)*
Howl thro' the dwelling o' the clerk![†] *(lawyer)*
May ne'er his gen'rous, honest heart,
For that same gen'rous spirit smart!
May Kennedy's far-honor'd name
Lang beet[†]his hymeneal flame, *(feed)*
Till Hamiltons, at least a dizzen,
Are frae their nuptial labors risen:
Five bonie lasses round their table,
And sev'n braw fellows, stout an' able,
To serve their king an' country weel,
By word, or pen, or pointed steel!
May Health and Peace, with mutual rays,
Shine on the ev'ning o' his days;
Till his wee, curlie John's ier-oe,[†] *(great-grandchild)*
When ebbing life nae mair shall flow,
The last, sad, mournful rites bestow!'

I will not wind a lang conclusion,
With complimentary effusion;
But, whilst your wishes and endeavours
Are blest with Fortune's smiles and favours,
I am, dear sir, with zeal most fervent,
Your much indebted, humble servant.

But if (which Pow'rs above prevent)
That iron-hearted carl, Want,
Attended, in his grim advances,
By sad mistakes, and black mischances,
While hopes, and joys, and pleasures fly him,
Make you as poor a dog as I am,
Your 'humble servant' then no more;
For who would humbly serve the poor?
But, by a poor man's hopes in Heav'n!
While recollection's pow'r is giv'n,
If, in the vale of humble life,
The victim sad of Fortune's strife,
I, thro' the tender-gushing tear,
Should recognize my master dear;
If friendless, low, we meet together,
Then, sir, your hand – my FRIEND and BROTHER!

TO A LOUSE

ON SEEING ONE ON A LADY'S BONNET AT CHURCH

1

Ha! whare ye gaun, ye crowlin ferlie?[†]   crawling
Your impudence protects you sairly,   wonder
I canna say but ye strunt[†]rarely   swagger
            Owre gauze and lace,
Tho' faith! I fear ye dine but sparely
            On sic a place.

2

Ye ugly, creepin, blastit wonner,[†]   marvel
Detested, shunn'd by saunt an' sinner,
How daur ye set your fit[†]upon her –   foot
            Sae fine a lady!
Gae somewhere else and seek your dinner
            On some poor body.

3

Off!; temples; squat
scramble

Swith!† in some beggar's hauffet†squattle:†
There ye may creep, and sprawl, and sprattle,†
Wi' ither kindred, jumping cattle,
        In shoals and nations;
Whare horn nor bane ne'er daur unsettle
        Your thick plantations.

4

keep
falderals

Now haud†you there! ye're out o' sight,
Below the fatt'rils,† snug an' tight;
Na, faith ye yet! ye'll no be right,
        Till ye've got on it –
The vera tapmost, tow'ring height
        O' Miss's bonnet.

5

gooseberry
rosin
deadly; powder

breech

My sooth! right bauld ye set your nose out,
As plump an' grey as onie grozet:†
O for some rank, mercurial rozet,†
        Or fell,† red smeddum,†
I'd gie ye sic a hearty dose o't,
        Wad dress your droddum!†

6

would not have
flannel cap
maybe; small ragged
undervest
balloon bonnet

I wad na†been surpris'd to spy
You on an auld wife's flainen toy;†
Or aiblins†some bit duddie†boy,
        On's wyliecoat;†
But Miss's fine Lunardi!† fye!
        How daur ye do't?

7

abroad

Those

O Jenny, dinna toss your head,
An' set your beauties a' abroad!†
Ye little ken what cursèd speed
        The blastie's makin!
Thae†winks an' finger-ends, I dread,
        Are notice takin!

8

O wad some Power the giftie gie us
To see oursels as others see us!
It wad frae monie a blunder free us,
        An' foolish notion:
What airs in dress an' gait wad lea'e us,
        An' ev'n devotion!

EPISTLE TO J. LAPRAIK

AN OLD SCOTTISH BARD,

April 1, 1785

1

While briers an' woodbines budding green,
And paitricks†scraichin†loud at e'en,   partridges; calling
An' morning poussie†whiddin†seen,   the hare;
         Inspire my Muse,   scudding
This freedom, in an unknown frien'
         I pray excuse.

2

On Fasten-e'en we had a rockin,†   meeting
To ca' the crack†and weave our stockin;   have a chat
And there was muckle fun and jokin,
         Ye need na doubt;
At length we had a hearty yokin,†   set-to
         At 'sang about.'

3

There was ae†sang, amang the rest,   one
Aboon†them a' it pleas'd me best,   Above
That some kind husband had addrest
         To some sweet wife:
It thirl'd†the heart-strings thro' the breast,   thrilled
         A' to the life.

4

I've scarce heard ought describ'd sae weel,
What gen'rous, manly bosoms feel;
Thought I, 'Can this be Pope or Steele,
         Or Beattie's wark?'
They tald me 'twas an odd kind chiel†   chap
         About Muirkirk.

[53]

5

tingling-wild   It pat me fidgin-fain†to hear't,
asked   An' sae about him there I spier't;†
   Then a' that kent him round declar'd
genius   He had ingine;†
   That nane excell'd it, few cam near't,
            It was sae fine:

6

   That, set him to a pint of ale,
sober   An' either douce†or merry tale,
   Or rhymes an' sangs he'd made himsel,
            Or witty catches,
   'Tween Inverness an' Teviotdale,
            He had few matches.

7

swore   Then up I gat, an' swoor†an aith,
harness   Tho' I should pawn my pleugh an' graith,†
hawker   Or die a cadger†pownie's death,
Behind a   At some dyke-back,†
    fence
   A pint an' gill I'd gie them baith,
talk   To hear your crack.†

8

   But, first an' foremost, I should tell,
   Amaist as soon as I could spell,
rhyming   I to the crambo-jingle†fell;
            Tho' rude an' rough –
humming   Yet crooning†to a body's sel,
            Does weel eneugh.

9

   I am nae poet, in a sense;
   But just a rhymer like by chance,
   An' hae to learning nae pretence;
            Yet, what the matter?
   Whene'er my Muse does on me glance,
            I jingle at her.

10

   Your critic-folk may cock their nose,
   And say, 'How can you e'er propose,
   You wha ken hardly verse frae prose,
            To mak a sang?'
   But, by your leaves, my learned foes,
            Ye're maybe wrang.

11

What's a' your jargon o' your Schools,
Your Latin names for horns an' stools?
If honest Nature made you fools,
   What sairs[†]your grammers?   serves
Ye'd better taen up spades and shools,[†]   shovels
   Or knappin[†]-hammers.   stone-
           breaking-

12

A set o' dull, conceited hashes[†]   dunderheads
Confuse their brains in college-classes,
They gang in stirks,[†] and come out asses,   young
   Plain truth to speak;   bullocks
An' syne[†]they think to climb Parnassus   then
   By dint o' Greek!

13

Gie me ae spark o' Nature's fire,
That's a' the learning I desire;
Then, tho' I drudge thro' dub[†]an' mire   puddle
   At pleugh or cart,
My Muse, tho' hamely in attire,
   May touch the heart.

14

O for a spunk[†]o' Allan's glee,   spark
Or Fergusson's, the bauld an' slee,[†]   sly
Or bright Lapraik's, my friend to be,
   If I can hit it!
That would be lear[†]eneugh for me,   learning
   If I could get it.

15

Now, sir, if ye hae friends enow,
Tho' real friends I b'lieve are few;
Yet, if your catalogue be fow,[†]   full
   I'se[†]no insist: I'll
But, gif[†]ye want ae friend that's true,   if
   I'm on your list.

16

I winna blaw[†]about mysel,   brag
As ill I like my fauts to tell;
But friends, an' folks that wish me well,
   They sometimes roose[†]me;   praise
Tho', I maun own, as monie still
   As far abuse me.

[55]

17

one   There's ae†wee faut they whyles lay to me,
God   I like the lasses – Gude†forgie me!
coin   For monie a plack†they wheedle frae me
                                  At dance or fair;
             Maybe some ither thing they gie me,
                                  They weel can spare.

18

             But Mauchline Race or Mauchline Fair,
             I should be proud to meet you there:
We'll   We'se†gie ae night's discharge to care,
                                  If we forgather;
             And hae a swap o' rhymin-ware
                                  Wi' ane anither.

19

four-gill cup,
  we'll make   The four-gill chap, we'se gar†him clatter,
christen; steaming An' kirsen†him wi' reekin†water;
Then; draught   Syne†we'll sit down an' tak our whitter,†
                                  To cheer our heart;
             An' faith, we'se be acquainted better
                                  Before we part.

20

worldly   Awa ye selfish, warly†race,
manners   Wha think that havins,† sense, an' grace,
             Ev'n love an' friendship should give place
the hunt for coin   To Catch-the-Plack!†
             I dinna like to see your face,
                                  Nor hear your crack.

21

             But ye whom social pleasure charms,
             Whose hearts the tide of kindness warms,
             Who hold your being on the terms,
                          'Each aid the others,'
             Come to my bowl, come to my arms,
                            My friends, my brothers!

22

             But, to conclude my lang epistle,
             As my auld pen's worn to the grissle,
make; tingle   Twa lines frae you wad gar†me fissle,†
                              Who am most fervent,
             While I can either sing or whistle,
                            Your friend and servant.

TO WILLIAM SIMPSON OF
OCHILTREE

May 1785

1

I gat your letter, winsome Willie;
Wi' gratefu' heart, I thank you brawlie;† handsomely
Tho' I maun say't, I wad be silly
    And unco†vain,   mighty
Should I believe, my coaxin billie,† fellow
    Your flatterin strain.

2

But I'se†believe ye kindly meant it: I'll
I sud be laith†to think ye hinted loath
Ironic satire, sidelins sklented,† sideways
    On my poor Musie;   squinted
Tho' in sic phraisin†terms ye've penn'd it, wheedling
    I scarce excuse ye.

3

My senses wad be in a creel,† tangle
Should I but dare a hope to speel,† climb
Wi' Allan,† or wi' Gilbertfield,† Ramsay;
    The braes o' fame; William
          Hamilton
Or Fergusson, the writer-chiel,† lawyer-chap
    A deathless name.

4

(O Fergusson! thy glorious parts
Ill suited law's dry, musty arts!
My curse upon your whunstane†hearts, granite
    Ye E'nbrugh gentry!
The tythe o' what ye waste at cartes
    Wad stow'd†his pantry!) Would have
            stored

[57]

5

Yet when a tale comes i' my head,
Or lasses gie my heart a screed[†]–
As whyles[†]they're like to be my dead,[†]
      (O sad disease!)
I kittle[†]up my rustic reed;
      It gies me ease.

rent
sometimes;
  death

tickle

6

Auld Coila,[†] now, may fidge fu' fain,[†]
She's gotten bardies o' her ain;
Chiels[†]wha their chanters[†]winna hain,[†]
      But tune their lays,
Till echoes a' resound again
      Her weel-sung praise.

Kyle; tingle
  with delight

lads;
  bagpipes;
  spare

7

Nae Poet thought her worth his while,
To set her name in measur'd style;
She lay like some unkend-of isle
      Beside New Holland.
Or whare wild-meeting oceans boil
      Besouth[†]Magellan.

South of

8

Ramsay an' famous Fergusson
Gied Forth an' Tay a lift aboon;[†]
Yarrow an' Tweed, to monie a tune,
      Owre Scotland rings;
While Irwin, Lugar, Ayr, an' Doon
      Naebody sings.

a lift-up

9

Th' Illissus, Tiber, Thames, an' Seine,
Glide sweet in monie a tunefu' line:
But, Willie, set your fit[†]to mine,
      An' cock your crest!
We'll gar[†]our streams and burnies[†]shine
      Up wi' the best.

foot

make;
  brooklets

10

We'll sing auld Coila's plains an' fells,
Her moors red-brown wi' heather bells,
Her banks an' braes,[†] her dens[†]an' dells,
      Whare glorious Wallace
Aft bure the gree,[†] as story tells,
      Frae Suthron billies.

hillsides;
  glens

bore off the
  prize

11

At Wallace' name, what Scottish blood
But boils up in a spring-tide flood?
Oft have our fearless fathers strode
      By Wallace' side,
Still pressing onward, red-wat-shod,[†]   red-wet-shod
      Or glorious dy'd!

12

O, sweet are Coila's haughs[†]an' woods,   hollows
When lintwhites[†]chant amang the buds,   linnets
And jinkin[†]hares, in amorous whids,[†]   sporting; gambols
      Their loves enjoy;
While thro' the braes the cushat[†]croods[†]   wild dove; coos
      With wailfu' cry!

13

Ev'n winter bleak has charms to me,
When winds rave thro' the naked tree;
Or frosts on hills of Ochiltree
      Are hoary gray;
Or blinding drifts wild-furious flee,
      Dark'ning the day!

14

O Nature! a' thy shews an' forms
To feeling, pensive hearts hae charms!
Whether the summer kindly warms,
      Wi' life an' light;
Or winter howls, in gusty storms,
      The lang, dark night!

15

The Muse, nae poet ever fand[†]her,   found
Till by himsel he learn'd to wander,
Adown some trottin[†]burn's[†]meander,   rippling; brook's
      An' no think lang:
O, sweet to stray, an' pensive ponder
      A heart-felt sang!

16

The warly[†]race may drudge an' drive,   worldly
Hog-shouther, jundie,[†] stretch, an' strive; push, ply the elbows
Let me fair Nature's face descrive,[†]   describe
      And I, wi' pleasure,
Shall let the busy, grumbling hive
      Bum[†]owre their treasure.   Hum

17

too long

May Envy wallop in a tether,[t]

dangle in a
rope

Fareweel, my rhyme-composing brither!
We've been owre lang[t]unkend to ither:
Now let us lay our heads thegither,
   In love fraternal:
May Envy wallop in a tether,[t]
   Black fiend, infernal!

18

accidentally
killed sheep

While Highlandmen hate tolls an' taxes;
While moorlan' herds like guid, fat braxies;[t]
While Terra Firma, on her axis,
   Diurnal turns;
Count on a friend, in faith an' practice,
   In Robert Burns.

POSTSCRIPT

19

pin

shepherds

My memory's no worth a preen:[t]
I had amaist forgotten clean,
Ye bade me write you what they mean
   By this New-Light,
'Bout which our herds[t]sae aft hae been
   Maist like to fight.

20

striplings

vernacular

In days when mankind were but callans;[t]
At grammar, logic, an' sic talents,
They took nae pains their speech to balance,
   Or rules to gie;
But spak their thoughts in plain, braid Lallans,[t]
   Like you or me.

21

those
shirt
round
Went

In thae[t]auld times, they thought the moon,
Just like a sark,[t] or pair o' shoon,
Wore by degrees, till her last roon[t]
   Gaed[t]past their viewin;
An' shortly after she was done,
   They gat a new ane.

22

fellows

This past for certain, undisputed;
It ne'er cam i' their heads to doubt it,
Till chiels[t]gat up an' wad confute it,
   An' ca'd it wrang;
An' muckle din there was about it,
   Baith loud an' lang.

23

Some herds, weel learn'd upo' the Beuk,
Wad threap†auld folk the thing misteuk;   maintain
For 'twas the auld moon turn'd a neuk†   corner
    An' out o' sight.
An' backlins-†comin to the leuk,†   backwards-;
    She grew mair bright.   look

24

This was deny'd, it was affirm'd;
The herds and hissels†were alarm'd;   flocks
The rev'rend gray-beards rav'd an' storm'd,
    That beardless laddies
Should think they better were inform'd
    Than their auld daddies.

25

Frae less to mair, it gaed to sticks;
Frae words an' aiths, to clours†an' nicks;†   bumps; cuts
An' monie a fallow gat his licks,†   punishment
    Wi' hearty crunt;†   blow
An' some, to learn†them for their tricks,   teach
    Were hang'd an' brunt.†   burned

26

This game was play'd in monie lands,
An' Auld-Light caddies†bure†sic hands,   varlets; bore
That faith, the youngsters took the sands
    Wi' nimble shanks
Till lairds forbade, by strict commands,
    Sic bluidy pranks.

27

But New-Light herds gat sic a cowe,†   down-setting
Folk thought them ruin'd stick-an-stowe;†   completely
Till now, amaist on ev'ry knowe†   hillock
    Ye'll find ane placed;
An' some, their New-Light fair avow,
    Just quite barefac'd.

28

Nae doubt the Auld-Light flocks are bleatin;
Their zealous herds are vex'd and sweatin;
Mysel, I've even seen them greetin†   weeping
    Wi' girnin†spite,   snarling
To hear the moon sae sadly lie'd on
    By word an' write.

29

scare; rascals

But shortly they will cowe†the louns!†
Some Auld-Light herds in neebor touns
Are mind't, in things they ca' balloons,
          To tak a flight,
An' stay ae month amang the moons
          An' see them right.

30

shard

pocket

Guid observation they will gie them;
An' when the auld moon's gaun to lea'e them,
The hindmost shaird,† they'll fetch it wi' them,
          Just i' their pouch;†
An' when the New-Light billies see them,
          I think they'll crouch!

31

squabble

such a brawl

Sae, ye observe that a' this clatter
Is naething but a 'moonshine matter';
But tho' dull prose-folk Latin splatter
          In logic tulzie,†
I hope we, Bardies, ken some better
          Than mind sic brulzie.†

EPISTLE TO JOHN RANKINE

ENCLOSING SOME POEMS

1

pick

O rough, rude, ready-witted Rankine,
The wale†o' cocks for fun an' drinkin!
There's monie godly folks are thinkin'
          Your dreams and tricks
Will send you, Korah-like, a-sinkin
          Straught to Auld Nick's.

2

Ye hae sae monie cracks†an' cants,　　　　　　stories
And in your wicked drucken rants,
Ye mak a devil o' the saunts,
　　　　　　An' fill them fou';
And then their failings, flaws, an' wants
　　　　　　Are a' seen thro'.

3

Hypocrisy, in mercy spare it!
That holy robe, O, dinna tear it!
Spare't for their sakes, wha aften wear it –
　　　　　　The lads in black;
But your curst wit, when it comes near it,
　　　　　　Rives't†aff their back.　　　　　　tears it

4

Think, wicked sinner, wha ye're skaithing;†　　injuring
It's just the Blue-gown badge†an' claithing　　licensed
O' saunts; tak that, ye lea'e them naething　　　　beggar
　　　　　　To ken them by
Frae onie unregenerate heathen,
　　　　　　Like you or I.

5

I've sent you here some rhyming ware
A' that I bargain'd for, an' mair;
Sae, when ye hae an hour to spare,
　　　　　　I will expect,
Yon sang ye'll sen't,† wi' cannie care,　　　　send it
　　　　　　And no neglect.

6

Tho' faith, sma' heart hae I to sing:
My Muse dow†scarcely spread her wing!　　　can
I've play'd mysel a bonie spring,†　　　　　tune
　　　　　　An' danc'd my fill!
I'd better gaen†an' sair't†the King　　　have gone;
　　　　　　At Bunker's Hill.　　　　　　served

7

'Twas ae night lately, in my fun,
I gaed†a rovin wi' the gun,　　　　　　went
An' brought a paitrick†to the grun' –　　partridge
　　　　　　A bonie hen;
And, as the twilight was begun,
　　　　　　Thought nane wad ken.

[63]

8

The poor, wee thing was little hurt;

stroked; a bit I straikit†it a wee†for sport,

worry Ne'er thinkin they wad fash†me for't;

But, Deil-ma-care!

the Kirk-Session Somebody tells the Poacher-Court†

whole The hale†affair.

9

Some auld, us'd hands had taen a note,

That sic a hen had got a shot;

I was suspected for the plot;

I scorn'd to lie;

lost my money So gat the whissle o' my groat,†

An' pay't the fee.

10

pick But, by my gun, o' guns the wale,†

shot An' by my pouther an' my hail,†

An' by my hen, an' by her tail,

I vow an' swear!

The game shall pay, owre moor an' dale,

next For this, niest†year!

11

clucking- As soon's the clockin†-time is by,

chicks An' the wee pouts†begun to cry,

I'll Lord, I'se†hae sportin by an' by

gold For my gowd†guinea;

Negro slaves Tho' I should herd the buckskin kye†

For't, in Virginia!

12

Trowth, they had muckle for to blame!

'Twas neither broken wing nor limb,

knocks; But twa-three chaps†about the wame,†

  belly Scarce thro' the feathers;

guinea An' baith a yellow George†to claim

endure; An' thole†their blethers!†

  nonsense

13

It pits me ay as mad's a hare;

So I can rhyme nor write nae mair;

tit-for-tat But pennyworths†again is fair,

When time's expedient:

Meanwhile I am, respected Sir,

Your most obedient.

DEATH AND DOCTOR HORNBOOK

A True Story

1

Some books are lies frae end to end,
And some great lies were never penn'd:
Ev'n ministers, they hae been kend,
   In holy rapture,
A rousing whid†at times to vend,   fib
   And nail't wi' Scripture.

2

But this that I am gaun†to tell,   going
Which lately on a night befel,
Is just as true's the Deil's in hell
   Or Dublin city:
That e'er he nearer comes oursel
   'S a muckle pity!

3

The clachan yill†had made me canty,†   village ale; jolly
I was na fou,† but just had plenty: drunk
I stacher'd whyles,† but yet took tent†ay   staggered now and
               then; care
   To free†the ditches;   clear
An' hillocks, stanes, an' bushes, kend ay
   Frae ghaists an' witches.

4

stare   The rising moon began to glowr[†]
above   The distant Cumnock Hills out-owre:[†]
     To count her horns, wi' a' my pow'r
         I set mysel;
     But whether she had three or four,
         I cou'd na tell.

5

     I was come round about the hill,
     And todlin down on Willie's mill,
     Setting my staff wi' a' my skill
steady   To keep me sicker;[†]
at times   Tho' leeward whyles,[†] against my will,
run   I took a bicker.[†]

6

did meet   I there wi' *Something* does forgather,[†]
put; ghostly dread   That pat[†]me in an eerie swither;[†]
across one   An awfu' scythe, out-owre ae[†]shouther,
hung   Clear-dangling, hang;[†]
three-pronged   A three-tae'd leister[†]on the ither
fish-spear   Lay, large an' lang.

7

ninety inches   Its stature seem'd lang Scotch ells twa;[†]
     The queerest shape that e'er I saw,
devil; belly; at all   For fient[†]a wame[†]it had ava;[†]
         And then its shanks,
     They were as thin, as sharp an' sma'
bridle ends   As cheeks o' branks.[†]

8

     'Guid-een,' quo' I; 'Friend! hae ye been mawin,
     When ither folk are busy sawin?'
halt   It seem'd to mak a kind o' stan',[†]
         But naething spak.
going   At length, says I: 'Friend! whare ye gaun?[†]
i.e. to the tavern   Will ye go back?'[†]

9

hollow   It spak right howe:[†] 'My name is Death,
scared   But be na' fley'd.'[†] Quoth I: 'Guid faith,
     Ye're may be come to stap my breath;
heed; comrade   But tent[†]me, billie:[†]
advise; damage   I red[†]ye weel, take care o' skaith,[†]
large knife   See, there's a gully!'[†]

10

'Gudeman,' quo' he, 'put up your whittle,†   *blade*
I'm no design'd to try its mettle;
But if I did, I wad be kittle†   *loath*
        To be mislear'd :†   *misinformed*
I wad na mind it, no that spittle
        Out-owre my beard.'

11

'Weel, weel!' says I, 'a bargain be't;
Come, gie's† your hand, an' say we're gree't;†   *give us; agreed*
We'll ease our shanks, an' tak a seat:
        Come, gie's your news:
This while ye hae been monie a gate,†   *road*
        At monie a house.'

12

'Ay, ay!' quo' he, an' shook his head,
'It's e'en a lang, lang time indeed
Sin' I began to nick† the thread   *cut*
        An' choke the breath:
Folk maun do something for their bread,
        An' sae maun Death.

13

'Sax thousand years are near-hand† fled   *well-nigh*
Sin' I was to the butching† bred,   *butchering*
An' monie a scheme in vain's been laid
        To stap† or scar† me;   *stop; scare*
Till ane Hornbook's ta'en up the trade,
        And faith! he'll waur† me.   *worst*

14

'Ye ken Jock Hornbook i' the clachan?†   *village*
Deil mak his king's-hood† in a spleuchan!†–   *scrotum; tobacco pouch*
He's grown sae weel acquaint wi' *Buchan*†   *William Buchan:*
        And ither chaps,   *Domestic Medicine*
The weans† haud out their fingers laughin,   *children*
        An' pouk my hips.

15

'See, here's a scythe, an' there's a dart,
They hae pierc'd monie a gallant heart;
But Doctor Hornbook wi' his art
        An' cursed skill,
Has made them baith no worth a fart,
        Damn'd haet† they'll kill!   *The devil a one*

16

gone

' 'Twas but yestreen, nae farther gane,†
I threw a noble throw at ane;
Wi' less, I'm sure, I've hundreds slain;
       But Deil-ma-care!

went tinkle

It just played dirl on the bane,†
       But did nae mair.

17

'Hornbook was by wi' ready art,
An' had sae fortify'd the part,
That when I lookèd to my dart,
       It was sae blunt,
Fient haet o't wad hae pierc'd the heart

cabbage-stalk

       Of a kail-runt.†

18

'I drew my scythe in sic a fury,

tumbled

I near-hand cowpit†wi' my hurry,
But yet the bauld Apothecary
       Withstood the shock:
I might as weel hae try'd a quarry
       O' hard whin-rock.

19

'Ev'n them he canna get attended,
Altho' their face he ne'er had kend it,

cabbage-leaf

Just shit in a kail-blade†an' send it,
       As soon's he smells't,
Baith their disease and what will mend it,
       At once he tells't.

20

knives

'And then a' doctor's saws and whittles†
Of a' dimensions, shapes, an' mettles,
A' kinds o' boxes, mugs, and bottles,
       He's sure to hae;
Their Latin names as fast he rattles
       As A B C.

21

'Calces o' fossils, earth, and trees;
True *sal-marinum* o' the seas;
The *farina* of beans an' pease,
       He has't in plenty;
Aqua-fontis, what you please,
       He can content ye.

'Forbye†some new, uncommon weapons,   Besides
Urinus spiritus of capons;
Or mite-horn shavings, filings, scrapings,
    Distill'd *per se*;
Sal-alkali o' midge-tail-clippings,
    And monie mae.'†   more

'Waes me for Johnie Ged's Hole†now,'   the grave
Quoth I, 'if that thae†news be true!   these
His braw calf-ward†whare gowans†grew grazing plot;
    Sae white and bonie,   daisies
Nae doubt they'll rive†it wi' the plew: split
    They'll ruin Johnie!'

The creature grain'd†an eldritch laugh,   groaned
And says: 'Ye nedna yoke the pleugh,
Kirkyards will soon be till'd eneugh,
    Tak ye nae fear:
They'll a' be trench'd wi monie a sheugh† ditch
    In twa-three year.

'Whare I kill'd ane, a fair strae†death straw,*i.e.*bed
By loss o' blood or want o' breath,
This night I'm free to tak my aith,
    That Hornbook's skill
Has clad a score i' their last claith†   cloth
    By drap an' pill.

'An honest wabster†to his trade,   weaver
Whase wife's twa nieves†were scarce weel-bred, fists
Gat tippence-worth to mend her head,
    When it was sair;†   aching
The wife slade cannie†to her bed, crept quietly
    But ne'er spak mair.

'A countra laird had taen the batts,†   diarrhoea
Or some curmurring†in his guts,   commotion
His only son for Hornbook sets,
    An' pays him well:
The lad, for twa guid gimmer-pets,†   pet-ewes
    Was laird himsel.

28

swelled; belly

'A bonie lass – ye kend her name –
Some ill-brewn drink had hov'd[†]her wame;[†]
She trusts hersel, to hide the shame,
            In Hornbook's care;
Horn sent her aff to her lang hame
            To hide it there.

29

sample

'That's just a swatch[†]o' Hornbook's way;
Thus goes he on from day to day,
Thus does he poison, kill, an' slay,
            An's weel paid for't;
Yet stops me o' my lawfu' prey
            Wi' his damn'd dirt:

30

'But, hark! I'll tell you of a plot,
Tho' dinna ye be speakin o't:
I'll nail the self-conceited sot,
            As dead's a herrin;

next; wager
comeuppance

Niest[†]time we meet, I'll wad[†]a groat,
            He gets his fairin!'[†]

31

But just as he began to tell,
The auld kirk-hammer strak the bell

small; beyond
      twelve

Some wee[†]short hour ayont the twal,[†]

got us to our legs

            Which raised us baith:[†]
I took the way that pleas'd mysel,
            And sae did Death.

THE BRIGS† OF AYR   bridges

A Poem

INSCRIBED TO

JOHN BALLANTINE, ESQ.,

AYR

The simple Bard, rough at the rustic plough,
Learning his tuneful trade from ev'ry bough
(The chanting linnet, or the mellow thrush,
Hailing the setting sun, sweet, in the green thorn
    bush;
The soaring lark, the perching red-breast shrill,
Or deep-ton'd plovers grey, wild-whistling o'er
    the hill):
Shall he – nurst in the peasant's lowly shed,
To hardy independence bravely bred,
By early poverty to hardship steel'd,
And train'd to arms in stern misfortune's field –
Shall he be guilty of their hireling crimes,
The servile, mercenary Swiss of rhymes?
Or labour hard the panegyric close,
With all the venal soul of dedicating prose?
No! though his artless strains he rudely sings,
And throws his hand uncouthly o'er the strings,
He glows with all the spirit of the bard,
Fame, honest fame, his great, his dear reward.
Still, if some patron's gen'rous care he trace,
Skill'd in the secret to bestow with grace;
When Ballantine befriends his humble name,
And hands the rustic stranger up to fame,
With heartfelt throes his grateful bosom swells:
The godlike bliss, to give, alone excels.

'Twas when the stacks get on their winter hap,†   wrap
And thack†and rape†secure the toil-won crap;†   thatch; rope; crop
Potatoe-bings†are snuggèd up frae skaith†   heaps; damage
O' coming winter's biting, frosty breath;
The bees, rejoicing o'er their summer toils –
Unnumber'd buds' an' flowers' delicious spoils,
Seal'd up with frugal care in massive waxen
    piles –
Are doom'd by man, that tyrant o'er the weak,
The death o' devils smoor'd†wi' brimstone reek:†   smothered; smoke
The thundering guns are heard on ev'ry side,
The wounded coveys, reeling, scatter wide;

[71]

The feather'd field-mates, bound by **Nature's** tie,
Sires, mothers, children, in one carnage lie:
(What warm, poetic heart but inly bleeds,
And execrates man's savage, ruthless deeds!)
Nae mair the flower in field or meadow springs;
Nae mair the grove with airy concert rings,
Except perhaps the robin's whistling glee,

<small half-grown> Proud o' the height o' some bit half-lang[†]tree;
The hoary morns precede the sunny days;
Mild, calm, serene, widespreads the noontide blaze,
While thick the gossamour waves wanton in the
      rays.

      'Twas in that season, when a simple Bard,
Unknown and poor – simplicity's reward! –

<One; burgh> Ae[†]night, within the ancient brugh[†] of Ayr,
By whim inspir'd, or haply prest wi' care,
He left his bed, and took his wayward route,
And down by Simpson's wheel'd the left about
(Whether impell'd by all-directing Fate,
To witness what I after shall narrate;
Or whether, rapt in meditation high,
He wander'd forth, he knew not where nor why):
The drowsy Dungeon-Clock had number'd two,
And Wallace Tower had sworn the fact was true;
The tide-swoln Firth, with sullen-sounding roar,
Through the still night dash'd hoarse along the
      shore;
All else was hush'd as Nature's closèd e'e;
The silent moon shone high o'er tower and tree;
The chilly frost, beneath the silver beam,
Crept, gently-crusting, o'er the glittering stream.

      When, lo! on either hand the list'ning Bard,

<swish> The clanging sugh[†]of whistling wings is heard;
Two dusky forms dart thro' the midnight air,

<hawk> Swift as the gos[†]drives on the wheeling hare;
Ane on th' Auld Brig his airy shape uprears,
The ither flutters o'er the rising piers:

<wizard> Our warlock[†]rhymer instantly descried
The Sprites that owre the Brigs of Ayr preside.
(That bards are second-sighted is nae joke,

<know> And ken[†]the lingo of the sp'ritual folk;
<jack-o'-lanterns, water-demons> Fays, spunkies, kelpies,[†] a', they can explain them,
<know them well> And ev'n the vera deils they brawly ken them[†]).

[72]

Auld Brig appear'd of ancient Pictish race,
The vera wrinkles Gothic in his face;
He seem'd as he wi' Time had warstl'd†lang,   wrestled
Yet, teughly doure,† he bade an unco bang.   toughly stubborn
New Brig was buskit†in a braw new coat,   dressed up
That he, at Lon'on, frae ane Adams got;
In's hand five taper staves as smooth's a bead.
Wi' virls†an' whirlygigums†at the head.   rings; flourishes
The Goth was stalking round with anxious
    search,
Spying the time-worn flaws in ev'ry arch.
It chanc'd his new-come neebor took his e'e,
And e'en a vex'd and angry heart had he!
Wi' thieveless†sneer to see his modish mien,   forbidding
He, down the water,† gies him this guid-een: –   river

AULD BRIG

'I doubt na, frien', ye'll think ye're nae sheep
    shank,†   'some pun'kins'
Ance ye were streekit owre†frae bank to bank!   stretched across
But gin†ye be a brig as auld as me –   when
Tho' faith, that date, I doubt, ye'll never see –
There'll be, if that day come, I'll wad a boddle,†   wager a farthing
Some fewer whigmeleeries†in your noddle.'   crotchets

NEW BRIG

'Auld Vandal! ye but show your little mense,†   discretion
Just much about it wi' your scanty sense:
Will your poor, narrow foot-path of a street,
Where twa wheel-barrows tremble when they meet,

[73]

Your ruin'd, formless bulk o' stane an' lime,
Compare wi' bonie brigs o' modern time?
There's men of taste would tak the Ducat
    stream,
Tho' they should cast the vera sark and swim,
E'er they would grate their feelings wi' the view
O' sic an ugly, Gothic hulk as you.'

AULD BRIG

       'Conceited gowk!† puff'd up wi' windy pride!
       This monie a year I've stood the flood an' tide;
       And tho' wi' crazy eild†I'm sair forfairn,†
       I'll be a brig when ye're a shapeless cairn!†
       As yet ye little ken about the matter,
       But twa-three†winters will inform ye better.
       When heavy, dark, continued, a'-day†rains
       Wi' deepening deluges o'erflow the plains;
       When from the hills where springs the brawling
           Coil,
       Or stately Lugar's mossy fountains boil,
       Or where the Greenock winds his moorland
           course,
       Or haunted Garpal draws his feeble source,
       Arous'd by blustering winds an' spotting thowes,†
       In monie a torrent down the snaw-broo rowes;†
       While crashing ice, borne on the roaring speat,†
       Sweeps dams, an' mills, an' brigs, a' to the gate;†
       And from Glenbuck down to the Ratton-Key
       Auld Ayr is just one lengthen'd, tumbling sea –
       Then down ye'll hurl†(deil nor ye never rise!),
       And dash the gumlie jaups†up to the pouring
           skies!
       A lesson sadly teaching, to your cost,
       That Architecture's noble art is lost!'

NEW BRIG

       'Fine architecture, trowth, I needs must say't
           o't,
       The Lord be thankit that we've tint the gate o't!†
       Gaunt, ghastly, ghaist-alluring edifices,
       Hanging with threat'ning jut, like precipices;
       O'er-arching, mouldy, gloom-inspiring coves,
       Supporting roofs fantastic – stony groves;
       Windows and doors in nameless sculptures drest,
       With order, symmetry, or taste unblest;

Marginal glosses: cuckoo; eld; worn out; pile of stones; two or three; day-long; thaws; slush rolls; flood; the road seaward; crash; muddy splashes; lost the trick

Forms like some bedlam statuary's dream,
The craz'd creations of misguided whim;
Forms might be worshipp'd on the bended knee,
And still the second dread Command be free:
Their likeness is not found on earth, in air, or
    sea!
Mansions that would disgrace the building taste
Of any mason reptile, bird or beast,
Fit only for a doited[†]monkish race,   muddled
Or frosty maids forsworn the dear embrace,
Or cuifs[†]of later times, wha held the notion,   dolts
That sullen gloom was sterling true devotion:
Fancies that our guid brugh denies protection,
And soon may they expire, unblest with
    resurrection!'

AULD BRIG

'O ye, my dear-remember'd, ancient yealings,[†]   coevals
Were ye but here to share my wounded feelings!
Ye worthy proveses,[†] an' monie a bailie,   provosts
Wha in the paths o' righteousness did toil ay;
Ye dainty deacons, an' ye douce[†]conveeners,   sedate
To whom our moderns are but causey[†]-cleaners; causeway-
Ye godly councils, wha hae blest this town;
Ye godly brethren o' the sacred gown,
Wha meekly gie your hurdies[†]to the smiters;   buttocks
And (what would now be strange), ye godly
    Writers;[†]   Lawyers
A' ye douce folk I've borne aboon[†]the broo,[†]   across;
Were ye but here, what would ye say or do!   water
How would your spirits groan in deep vexation
To see each melancholy alteration;
And, agonizing, curse the time and place
When ye begat the base degen'rate race!
Nae langer rev'rend men, their country's glory,
In plain braid Scots hold forth a plain, braid
    story;
Nae langer thrifty citizens, an' douce,
Meet owre a pint or in the council-house:
But staumrel,[†] corky-headed, graceless gentry, half-witted
The herryment[†]and ruin of the country;   spoliation
Men three-parts made by tailors and by barbers,
Wha waste your weel-hain'd gear[†]on damn'd   well-saved
    New Brigs and harbors!'   wealth

NEW BRIG

'Now haud you there! for faith ye've said
    enough,

make good   And muckle mair than ye can mak to through.†

As for your priesthood, I shall say but little,

ravens; sort; Corbies†and clergy are a shot†right kittle:†
ticklish

But, under favor o' your langer beard,

Abuse o' magistrates might weel be spar'd;

To liken them to your auld-warld squad,

I must needs say, comparisons are odd.

In Ayr, wag-wits nae mair can hae a handle

To mouth "a Citizen," a term o' scandal;

Nae mair the council waddles down the street,

In all the pomp of ignorant conceit;

haggling   Men wha grew wise priggin†owre hops an' raisins,

title deeds Or gather'd lib'ral views in bonds and seisins;†

If haply Knowledge, on a random tramp,

menaced   Had shor'd†them with a glimmer of his lamp,

And would to common-sense for once betray'd
    them,

Plain, dull stupidity stept kindly in to aid them.'

nonsense   What farther clish-ma-claver†might been said,

What bloody wars, if Sprites had blood to shed,

No man can tell; but, all before their sight,

A fairy train appear'd in order bright:

Adown the glittering stream they featly danc'd;

Bright to the moon their various dresses glanc'd;

They footed o'er the wat'ry glass so neat,

The infant ice scarce bent beneath their feet;

While arts of minstrelsy among them rung,

And soul-ennobling Bards heroic ditties sung.

(cat-)gut-   O, had M'Lauchlan, thairm†-inspiring sage,

Been there to hear this heavenly band engage,

When thro' his dear strathspeys they bore with
    Highland rage;

Or when they struck old Scotia's melting airs,

The lover's raptured joys or bleeding cares;

ear   How would his Highland lug†been nobler fir'd,

And ev'n his matchless hand with finer touch
    inspir'd!

No guess could tell what instrument appear'd,

But all the soul of Music's self was heard;

Harmonious concert rung in every part,
While simple melody pour'd moving on the heart.

   The Genius of the Stream in front appears,
A venerable chief advanc'd in years;
His hoary head with water-lilies crown'd,
His manly leg with garter-tangle bound.
Next came the loveliest pair in all the ring,
Sweet Female Beauty hand in hand with Spring;
Then, crown'd with flow'ry hay, came Rural Joy,
And Summer, with his fervid-beaming eye;
All-cheering Plenty, with her flowing horn,
Led yellow Autumn wreath'd with nodding
      corn;
Then Winter's time-bleach'd locks did hoary
      show,
By Hospitality, with cloudless brow.
Next follow'd Courage, with his martial stride,
From where the Feal wild-woody coverts hide;
Benevolence, with mild, benignant air,
A female form, came from the towers of Stair;
Learning and Worth in equal measures trode
From simple Catrine, their long-lov'd abode;
Last, white-rob'd Peace, crown'd with a hazel
      wreath,
To rustic Agriculture did bequeath
The broken, iron instruments of death:
At sight of whom our Sprites forgat their
      kindling wrath.

ADDRESS TO THE UNCO GUID

OR

THE RIGIDLY RIGHTEOUS

My son, these maxims make a rule,
An' lump them ay thegither:
The Rigid Righteous is a fool,
The Rigid Wise anither;
sifted   *The cleanest corn that e'er was dight†*
chaff   *May hae some pyles o' caff†in;*
So ne'er a fellow-creature slight
larking   *For random fits o' daffin.†*

SOLOMON (*Eccles.* vii. 16)

1

O ye, wha are sae guid yoursel,
    Sae pious and sae holy,
Ye've nought to do but mark and tell
    Your neebour's fauts and folly;
well-going   Whase life is like a weel-gaun†mill,
    Supplied wi' store o' water;
hopper   The heapet happer's†ebbing still,
clapper   An' still the clap†plays clatter!

2

company   Hear me, ye venerable core,†
    As counsel for poor mortals
sober   That frequent pass douce†Wisdom's door
giddy   For glaikit†Folly's portals:
I for their thoughtless, careless sakes
put forward   Would here propone†defences –
restive   Their donsie†tricks, their black mistakes,
    Their failings and mischances.

3

Ye see your state wi' theirs compared,
contrast   And shudder at the niffer;†
But cast a moment's fair regard,
    What makes the mighty differ?
Discount what scant occasion gave;
    That purity ye pride in;
rest   And (what's aft mair than a' the lave†)
    Your better art o' hidin.

4

Think, when your castigated pulse
    Gies now and then a wallop,

[78]

What ragings must his veins convulse,
 That still eternal gallop!
Wi' wind and tide fair i' your tail,
 Right on ye scud your sea-way;
But in the teeth o' baith to sail,
 It maks an unco[†]lee-way.   uncommon

5

See Social-life and Glee sit down
 All joyous and unthinking,
Till, quite transmugrify'd, they're grown
 Debauchery and Drinking:
O, would they stay to calculate,
 Th' eternal consequences,
Or – your more dreaded hell to state –
 Damnation of expenses!

6

Ye high, exalted, virtuous dames,
 Tied up in godly laces,
Before ye gie poor Frailty names,
 Suppose a change o' cases:
A dear-lov'd lad, convenience snug,
 A treach'rous inclination –
But, let me whisper i' your lug,[†]   ear
 Ye're aiblins[†]nae temptation.   maybe

7

Then gently scan your brother man,
 Still gentler sister woman;
Tho' they may gang a kennin wrang,[†]   go a trifle
 To step aside is human: wrong
One point must still be greatly dark,
 The moving *why* they do it;
And just as lamely can ye mark
 How far perhaps they rue it.

8

Who made the heart, 'tis He alone
 Decidedly can try us:
He knows each chord, its various tone,
 Each spring, its various bias:
Then at the balance let's be mute,
 We never can adjust it;
What's done we partly may compute,
 But know not what's resisted.

[79]

LAMENT OF
MARY, QUEEN OF SCOTS

ON THE APPROACH OF SPRING

1

Now Nature hangs her mantle green
    On every blooming tree,
And spreads her sheets o' daisies white
    Out o'er the grassy lea;
Now Phoebus cheers the crystal streams,
    And glads the azure skies:
But nought can glad the weary wight
    That fast in durance lies.

2

larks   Now laverocks†wake the merry morn,
    Aloft on dewy wing;
blackbird   The merle,† in his noontide bow'r,
    Makes woodland echoes ring;
The mavis wild wi' monie a note
    Sings drowsy day to rest:
In love and freedom they rejoice,
    Wi' care nor thrall opprest.

3

Now blooms the lily by the bank,
hill-side   The primrose down the brae;†

The hawthorn's budding in the glen,
   And milk-white is the slae:†   sloe
The meanest hind in fair Scotland
   May rove their sweets amang;
But I, the Queen of a' Scotland
   Maun†lie in prison strang.   must

4

I was the Queen o' bonie France,
   Where happy I hae been;
Fu' lightly rase I in the morn,
   As blythe lay down at e'en:
And I'm the sov'reign of Scotland,
   And monie a traitor there;
Yet here I lie in foreign bands
   And never-ending care.

5

But as for thee, thou false woman,
   My sister and my fae,†   foe
Grim vengeance yet shall whet a sword
   That thro' thy soul shall gae!†   go
The weeping blood in woman's breast
   Was never known to thee;
Nor th' balm that draps on wounds of woe
   Frae woman's pitying e'e.

6

My son! my son! may kinder stars
   Upon thy fortune shine;
And may those pleasures gild thy reign,
   That ne'er wad blink†on mine!   glance
God keep thee frae thy mother's faes,
   Or turn their hearts to thee;
And where thou meet'st thy mother's friend,
   Remember him for me!

7

O! soon, to me, may summer suns
   Nae mair light up the morn!
Nae mair to me the autumn winds
   Wave o'er the yellow corn!
And, in the narrow house of death,
   Let winter round me rave;
And the next flow'rs that deck the spring
   Bloom on my peaceful grave.

[81]

LAMENT FOR
JAMES, EARL OF GLENCAIRN

1

The wind blew hollow frae the hills;
   By fits the sun's departing beam
Look'd on the fading yellow woods,
   That wav'd o'er Lugar's winding stream.
craggy Beneath a craigy†steep a Bard,
much   Laden with years and meikle†pain,
In loud lament bewail'd his lord,
   Whom Death had all untimely taen.

2

oak He lean'd him to an ancient aik,†
   Whose trunk was mould'ring down with years;
His locks were bleachèd white with time,
   His hoary cheek was wet wi' tears;
And as he touch'd his trembling harp,
   And as he tun'd his doleful sang,
The winds, lamenting thro' their caves,
   To echo bore the notes alang: –

3

'Ye scatter'd birds that faintly sing,
   The reliques of the vernal quire!
Ye woods that shed on a' the winds
   The honors of the agèd year!
A few short months, and, glad and gay,
   Again ye'll charm the ear and e'e;
But nocht in all revolving time
   Can gladness bring again to me.

4

'I am a bending aged tree,
   That long has stood the wind and rain;

But now has come a cruel blast,
  And my last hold of earth is gane;
Nae leaf o' mine shall greet the spring,
  Nae simmer sun exalt my bloom;
But I maun lie before the storm,
  And ithers plant them in my room.

                5

'I've seen sae monie changefu' years,
  On earth I am a stranger grown:
I wander in the ways of men,
  Alike unknowing and unknown:
Unheard, unpitied, unreliev'd,
  I bear alane my lade⁺o' care;   load
For silent, low, on beds of dust,
  Lie a' that would my sorrows share.

                6

'And last (the sum of a' my griefs!)
  My noble master lies in clay;
The flow'r amang our barons bold,
  His country's pride, his country's stay:
In weary being now I pine,
  For a' the life of life is dead,
And hope has left my agèd ken,
  On forward wing for ever fled.

                7

'Awake thy last sad voice, my harp!
  The voice of woe and wild despair!
Awake, resound thy latest lay,
  Then sleep in silence evermair!
And thou, my last, best, only friend,
  That fillest an untimely tomb,
Accept this tribute from the Bard
  Thou brought from Fortune's mirkest gloom.

                8

'In Poverty's low barren vale,
  Thick mists obscure involv'd me round;
Though oft I turn'd the wistful eye,
  Nae ray of fame was to be found;
Thou found'st me, like the morning sun
  That melts the fogs in limpid air:
The friendless Bard and rustic song
  Became alike thy fostering care.

                [83]

9

'O, why has Worth so short a date,
　While villains ripen grey with time!
Must thou, the noble, gen'rous, great,
　Fall in bold manhood's hardy prime?
Why did I live to see that day,
　A day to me so full of woe?
O, had I met the mortal shaft
　Which laid my benefactor low!

10

'The bridegroom may forget the bride
　Was made his wedded wife yestreen;
The monarch may forget the crown
　That on his head an hour has been;
The mother may forget the child
　That smiles sae sweetly on her knee;
But I'll remember thee, Glencairn,
　And a' that thou hast done for me!'

TAM O' SHANTER

A Tale

Of Brownyis and of Bogillis full is this Buke.
GAWIN DOUGLAS

peddler fellows　　When chapman billies†leave the street,
thirsty　　And drouthy†neebors neebors meet;
　　As market-days are wearing late,
road　　An' folk begin to tak the gate;†
ale　　While we sit bousing at the nappy,†
full; mighty　　An' getting fou†and unco†happy,
not　　We think na†on the lang Scots miles,
bogs, pools,　　The mosses, waters, slaps,†and styles,†
　breaches;　　That lie between us and our hame,
　stiles　　Whare sits our sulky, sullen dame,
　　Gathering her brows like gathering storm,
　　Nursing her wrath to keep it warm.

found　　This truth fand†honest Tam o' Shanter,
one　　As he frae Ayr ae†night did canter:
　　(Auld Ayr, wham ne'er a town surpasses,
　　For honest men and bonie lasses).

[84]

O Tam, had'st thou but been sae wise,
As taen⁺thy ain wife Kate's advice!   *to have taken*
She tauld thee weel thou was a skellum,⁺   *good-for-nothing*
A blethering,⁺ blustering, drunken blellum;⁺   *chattering;*
That frae November till October,   *babbler*
Ae market-day thou was nae sober;
That ilka melder⁺wi' the miller,   *meal-grinding*
Thou sat as lang as thou had siller;⁺   *money*
That ev'ry naig was ca'd a shoe on,⁺   *needed shoeing*
The smith and thee gat roaring fou⁺on;   *full*
That at the Lord's house, even on Sunday,
Thou drank wi' Kirkton Jean till Monday.
She prophesied, that, late or soon,
Thou would be found deep drown'd in Doon,
Or catch'd wi' warlocks⁺in the mirk⁺   *wizards; dark*
By Alloway's auld, haunted kirk.

Ah! gentle dames, it gars⁺me greet,⁺   *makes; weep*
To think how monie counsels sweet,
How monie lengthen'd, sage advices
The husband frae the wife despises!

But to our tale: – Ae market-night,
Tam had got planted unco⁺right,   *uncommonly*
Fast by an ingle, bleezing⁺finely,   *fire, blazing*
Wi' reaming swats,⁺ that drank divinely;   *foaming new ale*
And at his elbow, Souter⁺Johnie,   *Cobbler*
His ancient, trusty, drouthy cronie:
Tam lo'ed him like a very brither;
They had been fou for weeks thegither.
The night drave on wi' sangs and clatter;
And ay the ale was growing better:
The landlady and Tam grew gracious
Wi' secret favors, sweet and precious:
The Souter tauld his queerest stories;
The landlord's laugh was ready chorus:
The storm without might rair⁺and rustle,   *roar*
Tam did na mind the storm a whistle.

Care, mad to see a man sae happy,
E'en drown'd himsel amang the nappy.
As bees flee hame wi' lades o' treasure,
The minutes wing'd their way wi' pleasure:
Kings may be blest but Tam was glorious,
O'er a' the ills o' life victorious!

But pleasures are like poppies spread:
You seize the flow'r, its bloom is shed;
Or like the snow falls in the river,
A moment white – then melts for ever;
Or like the borealis race,
That flit ere you can point their place;
Or like the rainbow's lovely form
Evanishing amid the storm.
Nae man can tether time or tide;
The hour approaches Tam maun†ride: *must*
That hour, o' night's black arch the key-stane,
That dreary hour Tam mounts his beast in;
And sic a night he taks the road in,
As ne'er poor sinner was abroad in.

The wind blew as 'twad†blawn its last;   *would have*
The rattling showers rose on the blast;
The speedy gleams the darkness swallow'd;
Loud, deep, and lang the thunder bellow'd:
That night, a child might understand,
The Deil had business on his hand.

Weel mounted on his gray mare Meg,
A better never lifted leg,
Tam skelpit†on thro' dub†and mire,   *splashed; puddle*
Despising wind, and rain, and fire;
Whiles†holding fast his guid blue bonnet,   *Now*
Whiles crooning o'er some auld Scots sonnet,†   *song*
Whiles glow'ring†round wi' prudent cares,   *staring*
Lest bogles†catch him unawares: *bogies*
Kirk-Alloway was drawing nigh,
Whare ghaists and houlets†nightly cry.   *owls*

By this time he was cross†the ford,   *across*
Whare in the snaw the chapman smoor'd;†   *smothered*
And past the birks†and meikle†stane,   *birches; big*
Whare drunken Charlie brak's neck-bane;
And thro' the whins,† and by the cairn,†   *furze; pile of stones*
Whare hunters fand the murder'd bairn;
And near the thorn, aboon†the well,   *above*
Whare Mungo's mither hang'd hersel.
Before him Doon pours all his floods;
The doubling storm roars thro' the woods;
The lightnings flash from pole to pole;
Near and more near the thunders roll:

[86]

When, glimmering thro' the groaning trees,
Kirk-Alloway seem'd in a bleeze,
Thro' ilka bore†the beams were glancing,   every chink
And loud resounded mirth and dancing.

    Inspiring bold John Barleycorn,
What dangers thou canst make us scorn!
Wi' tippenny,† we fear nae evil;   ale
Wi' usquabae,† we'll face the Devil!   whisky
The swats sae ream'd in Tammie's noddle,
Fair play, he car'd na†deils a boddle.†   not; farthing
But Maggie stood, right sair astonish'd,
Till, by the heel and hand admonish'd,
She ventur'd forward on the light;
And, vow! Tam saw an unco†sight!   wondrous

    Warlocks and witches in a dance:
Nae cotillion, brent†new frae France,   brand
But hornpipes, jigs, strathspeys, and reels,
Put life and mettle in their heels.
A winnock-bunker†in the east,   window-seat
There sat Auld Nick, in shape o' beast;
A tousie tyke,† black, grim, and large,   shaggy dog
To gie them music was his charge:
He screw'd the pipes and gart them skirl,†   squeal
Till roof and rafters a' did dirl.†   ring
Coffins stood round, like open presses,†   cupboards
That shaw'd the dead in their last dresses;

magic device	And, by some devilish cantraip sleight,[†]
	Each in its cauld hand held a light:
	By which heroic Tam was able
	To note upon the haly table,
-irons	A murderer's banes, in gibbet-airns;[†]
	Twa span-lang, wee, unchristen'd bairns;
	A thief new-cutted frae a rape –
mouth	Wi' his last gasp his gab[†]did gape;
	Five tomahawks wi' bluid red-rusted;
	Five scymitars wi' murder crusted;
	A garter which a babe had strangled;
	A knife a father's throat had mangled –
	Whom his ain son o' life bereft –
	The grey-hairs yet stack to the heft;
	Wi' mair of horrible and awefu',
	Which even to name wad be unlawfu'.

stared	As Tammie glowr'd,[†] amaz'd, and curious,
	The mirth and fun grew fast and furious;
	The piper loud and louder blew,
	The dancers quick and quicker flew,
took hold	They reel'd, they set, they cross'd, they cleekit,[†]
beldam sweated and steamed	Till ilka carlin swat and reekit,[†]
doffed; rags; work	And coost[†]her duddies[†]to the wark,[†]
tripped; shift	And linket[†]at it in her sark![†]

these	Now Tam, O Tam! had thae[†]been queans,
	A' plump and strapping in their teens!
greasy	Their sarks, instead o' creeshie[†]flannen,
	Been snaw-white seventeen hunder linen! –
These	Thir[†]breeks o' mine, my only pair,
	That ance were plush, o' guid blue hair,
buttocks	I wad hae gi'en them off my hurdies[†]
maidens	For ae blink o' the bonie burdies![†]

	But wither'd beldams, auld and droll,
wean	Rigwoodie hags wad spean[†]a foal,
leaping; kicking; broomstick	Louping[†]and flinging[†]on a crummock,[†]
	I wonder did na turn thy stomach!

well	But Tam kend what was what fu' brawlie:[†]
comely; choice	There was ae winsome[†]wench and wawlie,[†]
company	That night enlisted in the core,[†]
	Lang after kend on Carrick shore

(For monie a beast to dead[†]she shot,   death
An' perish'd monie a bonie boat,
And shook baith meikle corn[†]and bear,[†] much oats;
And kept the country-side in fear).   barley
Her cutty sark,[†] o' Paisley harn,[†] short shift;
That while a lassie she had worn,   coarse cloth
In longitude tho' sorely scanty,
It was her best, and she was vauntie[†]. . . . proud
Ah! little kend thy reverend grannie,
That sark she coft[†]for her wee Nannie, bought
Wi' twa pund Scots ('twas a' her riches),
Wad[†]ever grac'd a dance of witches! Would have

But here my Muse her wing maun cour,[†] stoop
Sic flights are far beyond her power:
To sing how Nannie lap and flang[†] leaped and
(A souple jad she was and strang),   kicked
And how Tam stood like ane bewitch'd,
And thought his very een enrich'd;
Even Satan glowr'd, and fidg'd[†]fu' fain,[†] fidgeted; fond
And hotch'd[†]and blew wi' might and main; jerked
Till first ae caper, syne[†]anither,   then
Tam tint[†]his reason a' thegither,   lost
And roars out: 'Weel done, Cutty-sark!'
And in an instant all was dark;
And scarcely had he Maggie rallied,
When out the hellish legion sallied.

fret   As bees bizz out wi' angry fyke,†

hive   When plundering herds assail their byke;†

the hare's   As open pussie's†mortal foes,

When, pop! she starts before their nose;

As eager runs the market-crowd,

When 'Catch the thief!' resounds aloud:

So Maggie runs, the witches follow,

unearthly   Wi' monie an eldritch†skriech and hollo.

come-   Ah, Tam! Ah, Tam! thou'll get thy fairin!†
uppance

In hell they'll roast thee like a herrin!

In vain thy Kate awaits thy comin!

Kate soon will be a woefu' woman!

Now, do thy speedy utmost, Meg,

And win the key-stane of the brig;

There, at them thou thy tail may toss,

A running stream they dare na cross!

But ere the key-stane she could make,

devil   The fient†a tail she had to shake;

For Nannie, far before the rest,

Hard upon noble Maggie prest,

intent   And flew at Tam wi' furious ettle;†

But little wist she Maggie's mettle!

whole   Ae spring brought off her master hale,†

But left behind her ain grey tail:

seized   The carlin claught†her by the rump,

And left poor Maggie scarce a stump.

Now, wha this tale o' truth shall read,

Ilk man, and mother's son, take heed:

Whene'er to drink you are inclin'd,

Or cutty sarks run in your mind,

Think! ye may buy the joys o'er dear:

Remember Tam o' Shanter's mare.

ON THE LATE
CAPTAIN GROSE'S PEREGRINATIONS
THRO' SCOTLAND

COLLECTING THE ANTIQUITIES
OF THAT KINGDOM

1

Hear, Land o' Cakes, and brither Scots
Frae Maidenkirk to Johnie Groat's,
If there's a hole in a' your coats,
   I rede†you tent†it: advise; look to
A chield's†amang you takin notes,   fellow
   And faith he'll prent it:

2

If in your bounds ye chance to light
Upon a fine, fat, fodgel†wight,   dumpy
O' stature short but genius bright,
   That's he, mark weel:
And wow! he has an unco sleight†   skill
   O' cauk and keel.†   In chalk and
           red ocher

3

By some auld, houlet†-haunted biggin,†   owl-; dwelling
Or kirk deserted by its riggin,†   roof
It's ten to ane ye'll find him snug in
   Some eldritch†part,   fearsome
Wi' deils, they say, Lord safe's!† colleaguin   save us
   At some black art.

4

Ilk†ghaist that haunts auld ha' or chamer,†   Each; chamber
Ye gipsy-gang that deal in glamour,
And you, deep-read in hell's black grammar,
   Warlocks and witches:
Ye'll quake at his conjúring hammer,
   Ye midnight bitches!

5

It's tauld he was a sodger bred,
And ane wad[†]rather fa'n than fled;
But now he's quat[†]the spurtle-blade[†]
    And dog-skin wallet,
And taen the – Antiquarian trade,
    I think they call it.

would have
quitted; pot-stick (= sword)

6

He has a fouth[†]o' auld nick-nackets:
Rusty airn[†]caps and jinglin jackets
Wad haud the Lothians three in tackets[†]
    A towmont[†]guid;
And parritch-pats[†]and auld saut-backets[†]
    Before the Flood.

abundance
iron
shoenails
twelvemonth
porridge-pots; salt-boxes

7

Of Eve's first fire he has a cinder;
Auld Tubalcain's fire-shool[†]and fender;
That which distinguishèd the gender
    O' Balaam's ass;
A broomstick o' the witch of Endor,
    Weel shod wi' brass.

shovel

8

Forbye,[†] he'll shape you aff fu' gleg[†]
The cut of Adam's philibeg;[†]
The knife that nicket[†]Abel's craig[†]
    He'll prove you fully,
It was a faulding jocteleg,[†]
    Or lang-kail gullie.[†]

Besides; smartly
kilt
slit; throat
a clasp knife
cabbage knife

9

But wad ye see him in his glee –
For meikle[†]glee and fun has he –
Then set him down, and twa or three
    Guid fellows wi' him;
And port, O port! shine thou a wee,
    And then ye'll see him!

much

10

Now, by the Pow'rs o' verse and prose!
Thou art a dainty chield, O Grose! –
Whae'er o' thee shall ill suppose,
    They sair misca' thee;
I'd take the rascal by the nose,
    Wad say, 'Shame fa'[†]thee.'

befall

THE JOLLY BEGGARS

A Cantata

RECITATIVO

1

When lyart†leaves bestrow the yird,†	withered; ground
Or, wavering like the bauckie-bird,†	bat
Bedim cauld Boreas' blast;	
When hailstanes drive wi' bitter skyte,†	lash
And infant frosts begin to bite,	
In hoary cranreuch†drest;	rime
Ae†night at e'en a merry core†	One; gang
O' randie, gangrel†bodies	lawless, vagrant
In Poosie-Nansie's held the splore,†	carousal
To drink their orra duddies:†	spare rags
Wi' quaffing and laughing	
They ranted†an' they sang,	roistered
Wi' jumping an' thumping	
The vera girdle†rang.	griddle

2

First, niest†the fire, in auld red rags	next
Ane sat, weel brac'd wi' mealy bags†	haversack
And knapsack a' in order;	
His doxy lay within his arm;	
Wi' usquebae†an' blankets warm,	whisky
She blinket†on her sodger.	leered
An' ay he gies the tozie†drab	flushed with drink
The tither skelpin†kiss,	sounding
While she held up her greedy gab†	mouth
Just like an aumous dish:†	alms-dish
Ilk†smack still did crack still	Each
Like onie cadger's†whup;	hawker's
Then, swaggering an' staggering,	
He roar'd this ditty up: –	

AIR

TUNE: *Soldier's Joy*

1

I am a son of Mars, who have been in many wars,
 And show my cuts and scars wherever I come:
This here was for a wench, and that other in a
  trench
 When welcoming the French at the sound of
  the drum.

        Lal de daudle, *etc.*

2

My prenticeship I past, where my leader
  breath'd his last,
 When the bloody die was cast on the heights of
  Abram;
And I servèd out my trade when the gallant
  game was play'd,
 And the Moro low was laid at the sound of the
  drum.

3

I lastly was with Curtis among the floating
  batt'ries,
 And there I left for witness an arm and a limb;
Yet let my country need me, with Eliott to head
  me
 I'd clatter on my stumps at the sound of the
  drum.

4

And now, tho' I must beg with a wooden arm
  and leg
 And many a tatter'd rag hanging over my bum,
I'm as happy with my wallet, my bottle, and my
trull   callet[†]
 As when I us'd in scarlet to follow a drum.

5

What tho' with hoary locks I must stand the
  winter shocks,
 Beneath the woods and rocks oftentimes for a
  home?
When the tother bag I sell, and the tother bottle
  tell,
 I could meet a troop of Hell at the sound of a
  drum.

        Lal de daudle, *etc.*

RECITATIVO

He ended; and the kebars sheuk†   rafters shook
    Aboon†the chorus roar;   Over
While frighted rattons†backward leuk,   rats
    An' seek the benmost bore:†   inmost hole
A fairy†fiddler frae the neuk,†   tiny; corner
    He skirl'd†out *Encore!*   squeaked
But up arose the martial chuck,†   dear
    An' laid the loud uproar: –

AIR
TUNE: *Sodger Laddie*

1

I once was a maid, tho' I cannot tell when,
And still my delight is in proper young men.
Some one of a troop of dragoons was my daddie:
No wonder I'm fond of a sodger laddie!
                Sing, lal de dal, *etc.*

2

The first of my loves was a swaggering blade:
To rattle the thundering drum was his trade;
His leg was so tight, and his cheek was so ruddy,
Transported I was with my sodger laddie.

3

But the godly old chaplain left him in the lurch;
The sword I forsook for the sake of the church;
He riskèd the soul, and I ventur'd the body:
'Twas then I prov'd false to my sodger laddie.

4

Full soon I grew sick of my sanctified sot;
The regiment at large for a husband I got;
From the gilded spontoon to the fife I was ready:
I askèd no more but a sodger laddie.

5

But the Peace it reduc'd me to beg in despair,
Till I met my old boy in a Cunningham Fair;
His rags regimental they flutter'd so gaudy:
My heart it rejoic'd at a sodger laddie.

6

And now I have liv'd – I know not how long!
But still I can join in a cup and a song;
And whilst with both hands I can hold the glass
    steady,
Here's to thee, my hero, my sodger laddie!
                Sing, lal de dal, *etc.*

[95]

RECITATIVO

Poor Merry-Andrew in the neuk
    Sat guzzling wi' a tinkler-hizzie;[†]
They mind't[†]na wha the chorus teuk,[†]
    Between themselves they were sae busy.
At length, wi' drink an' courting dizzy,
He stoiter'd[†]up an' made a face;
    Then turn'd an' laid a smack on Grizzie,
Syne[†]tun'd his pipes wi' grave grimace: –

Side glosses: tinker-wench / cared not; took / struggled / Then

AIR

Tune: *Auld Sir Symon*

1

Sir Wisdom's a fool when he's fou;[†]
    Sir Knave is a fool in a session:[†]
He's there but a prentice I trow,
    But I am a fool by profession.

Side glosses: drunk / court

2

My grannie she bought me a beuk,[†]
    An' I held awa[†]to the school:
I fear I my talent misteuk,
    But what will ye hae of a fool?

Side glosses: book / went off

3

For drink I wad venture my neck;
    A hizzie's the half of my craft:
But what could ye other expect
    Of ane that's avowedly daft?[†]

Side glosses: cracked

4

I ance was tyed up like a stirk[†]
    For civilly swearing and quaffing;
I ance was abus'd[†]i' the kirk
    For towsing[†]a lass i' my daffin.[†]

Side glosses: bullock / rebuked / rumpling; fun

5

Poor Andrew that tumbles for sport
    Let naebody name wi' a jeer:
There's even, I'm tauld, i' the Court
    A tumbler ca'd the Premier.

6

Observ'd ye yon reverend lad
    Mak faces to tickle the mob?
He rails at our mountebank squad –
    It's rivalship just i' the job!

[96]

And now my conclusion I'll tell,
   For faith! I'm confoundedly dry:
The chiel⁺that's a fool for himsel,   fellow
   Guid Lord! he's far dafter than I.

RECITATIVO

Then niest outspak a raucle carlin,⁺   sturdy beldam
Wha kent fu' weel to cleek the sterlin,⁺   pick pockets
For monie a pursie she had hookèd,
An' had in monie a well been doukèd.⁺   ducked
Her love had been a Highland laddie,
But weary fa'⁺the waefu' woodie!⁺   plague upon;
                                  gallows
Wi' sighs an' sobs she thus began
To wail her braw⁺John Highlandman: –   fine

AIR
Tune: *O, An' Ye Were Dead, Guidman*

1

A Highland lad my love was born,
The lalland⁺laws he held in scorn,   lowland
But he still was faithfu' to his clan,
My gallant, braw John Highlandman.

Chorus

Sing hey my braw John Highlandman!
Sing ho my braw John Highlandman!
There's not a lad in a' the lan'
Was match for my John Highlandman!

2

With his philibeg,⁺an' tartan plaid,   kilt
An' guid claymore⁺down by his side,   broad-sword
The ladies' hearts he did trepan,
My gallant, braw John Highlandman.

3

We rangèd a' from Tweed to Spey,
An' liv'd like lords an' ladies gay,
For a lalland face he fearèd none,
My gallant, braw John Highlandman.

4

They banish'd him beyond the sea,
But ere the bud was on the tree,
Adown my cheeks the pearls ran,
Embracing my John Highlandman.

5

But, Och! they catch'd him at the last,
And bound him in a dungeon fast.
My curse upon them every one –
They've hang'd my braw John Highlandman!

6

And now a widow I must mourn
The pleasures that will ne'er return;
No comfort but a hearty can
When I think on John Highlandman.

Chorus

Sing hey my braw John Highlandman!
Sing ho my braw John Highlandman!
There's not a lad in a' the lan'
Was match for my John Highlandman!

RECITATIVO

1

A pigmy scraper on a fiddle,
toddle   Wha us'd to trystes an' fairs to driddle,†
buxom   Her strappin limb an' gawsie†middle
       (He reach'd nae higher)
Had hol'd his heartie like a riddle,
blown it   An' blawn't†on fire.

2

hip   Wi' hand on hainch†and upward e'e,
hummed   He croon'd†his gamut, one, two, three,
Then in an *arioso* key
       The wee Apollo
Set off wi' *allegretto* glee
       His *giga* solo: –

AIR

rest   TUNE: *Whistle Owre the Lave*†*O't*

1

reach; wipe   Let me ryke†up to dight†that tear;
An' go wi' me an' be my dear,
An' then your every care an' fear
       May whistle owre the lave o't.

Chorus

I am a fiddler to my trade,
An' a' the tunes that e'er I play'd,

The sweetest still to wife or maid
Was *Whistle Owre the Lave O't.*

2

At kirns†an' weddins we'se†be there,   harvest-homes;
An' O, sae nicely's we will fare!   we'll
We'll bowse about till Daddie Care
    Sing *Whistle Owre the Lave O't.*

3

Sae merrily the banes†we'll pyke,†   bones; pick
An' sun oursels about the dyke;†   fence
An' at our leisure, when ye like,
    We'll – whistle owre the lave o't!

4

But bless me wi' your heav'n o' charms,
An' while I kittle†hair on thairms,†   tickle; catgut
Hunger, cauld, an' a' sic†harms   such
    May whistle owre the lave o't.

Chorus

I am a fiddler to my trade,
An' a' the tunes that e'er I play'd,
The sweetest still to wife or maid
    Was *Whistle Owre the Lave O't.*

RECITATIVO

1

Her charms had struck a sturdy caird†   tinker
    As weel as poor gut-scraper;
He taks the fiddler by the beard,
    An' draws a roosty†rapier;   rusty
He swoor by a' was swearing worth
    To speet him like a pliver,†   plover
Unless he would from that time forth
    Relinquish her for ever.

2

Wi' ghastly e'e poor Tweedle-Dee
    Upon his hunkers†bended,   hams
An' pray'd for grace wi' ruefu' face,
    An' sae†the quarrel ended.   so
But tho' his little heart did grieve
    When round the tinkler prest her,
He feign'd to snirtle†in his sleeve   snigger
    When thus the caird address'd her: –

AIR

Patch   TUNE: *Clout† the Cauldron*

1

My bonie lass, I work in brass,
    A tinkler is my station;
I've travell'd round all Christian ground
    In this my occupation;
I've taen the gold, an' been enrolled
    In many a noble squadron;
But vain they search'd when off I march'd
    To go an' clout the cauldron.

2

Despite that shrimp, that wither'd imp,
    With a' his noise an' cap'rin,
An' take a share wi' those that bear
    The budget and the apron!

pot   And by that stowp,† my faith an' houpe!
whisky   And by that dear Kilbaigie!†
scarcity   If e'er ye want, or meet wi' scant,†
wet; throat   May I ne'er weet†my craigie!†

RECITATIVO

1

The caird prevail'd: th' unblushing fair
    In his embraces sunk,
Partly wi' love o'ercome sae sair,
    An' partly she was drunk.
Sir Violino, with an air
spirit   That show'd a man o' spunk,†
Wish'd unison between the pair,
    An' made the bottle clunk
            To their health that night.

2

urchin   But hurchin†Cupid shot a shaft,
trick   That play'd a dame a shavie:†
                The fiddler rak'd her fore and aft
hencoop   Behint the chicken cavie;†
chap   Her lord, a wight†of Homer's craft,
spavin   Tho' limpin' wi' the spavie,†
hobbled; leapt like mad   He hirpl'd†up, an' lap like daft,†
offered   An' shor'd†them 'Dainty Davie'
gratis   O' boot†that night.

3

He was a care-defying blade
　　As ever Bacchus listed!
Tho’ Fortune sair upon him laid,
　　His heart, she ever miss’d it.
He had no wish but – to be glad,
　　Nor want but – when he thristed,
He hated nought but – to be sad;
　　An’ thus the Muse suggested
　　　　His sang that night.

AIR

Tune: *For A’ That, an’ A’ That*

1

I am a Bard, of no regard
　　Wi’ gentle folks an’ a’†that,　　　　　　and all
But Homer-like the glowrin byke,†　　　　staring crowd
　　Frae town to town I draw that.

Chorus

　　For a’ that, an’ a’ that,
　　　　An’ twice as muckle’s†a’ that,　　　much
　　I’ve lost but ane, I’ve twa behin’,
　　　　I’ve wife eneugh for a’ that.

2

I never drank the Muses’ stank,†　　　　　pond
　　Castalia’s burn,† an’ a’ that;　　　　　brook
But there it streams, an’ richly reams†–　foams
　　My Helicon I ca’ that.

3

Great love I bear to a’ the fair,
　　Their humble slave an’ a’ that;
But lordly will, I hold it still
　　A mortal sin to thraw†that.　　　　　　thwart

4

In raptures sweet this hour we meet
　　Wi’ mutual love an’ a’ that;
But for how lang the flie†may stang,†　　　fly; sting
　　Let inclination law that!

5

Their tricks an’ craft hae put me daft,
　　They’ve taen me in, an’ a’ that;

[101]

But clear your decks, an' here's the Sex!
I like the jads for a' that.

Chorus

For a' that, an' a' that,
An' twice as muckle's a' that,
My dearest bluid, to do them guid,
to it They're welcome till't[†]for a' that!

RECITATIVO

walls So sung the Bard, and Nansie's wa's[†]
Shook with a thunder of applause,
Re-echo'd from each mouth!
emptied They toom'd their pocks,[†] they pawn'd their
   their bags duds,
cover; tails They scarcely left to coor[†]their fuds,[†]
burning To quench their lowin[†]drouth.
company Then owre again the jovial thrang[†]
The Poet did request
untie; To lowse[†]his pack, an' wale[†]a sang,
   choose A ballad o' the best:
He rising, rejoicing
Between his twa Deborahs,
Looks round him, an' found them
Impatient for the chorus: –

AIR
TUNE: *Jolly Mortals, Fill Your Glasses*

1

See the smoking bowl before us!
Mark our jovial, ragged ring!
Round and round take up the chorus,
And in raptures let us sing:

Chorus

A fig for those by law protected!
Liberty's a glorious feast,
Courts for cowards were erected,
Churches built to please the priest!

2

What is title, what is treasure,
What is reputation's care?
If we lead a life of pleasure,
'Tis no matter how or where!

3

With the ready trick and fable
  Round we wander all the day;
And at night in barn or stable
  Hug our doxies on the hay.

4

Does the train-attended carriage
  Thro' the country lighter rove?
Does the sober bed of marriage
  Witness brighter scenes of love?

5

Life is all a variorum,
  We regard not how it goes;
Let them prate about decorum,
  Who have character to lose.

6

Here's to budgets, bags, and wallets!
  Here's to all the wandering train!
Here's our ragged brats and callets!
  One and all, cry out, Amen!

Chorus

A fig for those by law protected!
  Liberty's a glorious feast,
Courts for cowards were erected,
  Churches built to please the priest!

HOLY WILLIE'S PRAYER

And send the godly in a pet to pray.

POPE

1

O Thou that in the Heavens does dwell,
Wha, as it pleases best Thysel,
Sends ane to Heaven an' ten to Hell
    A' for Thy glory,
And no for onie guid or ill
    They've done before Thee!

2

I bless and praise Thy matchless might,
When thousands Thou has left in night,
That I am here before Thy sight,
    For gifts an' grace
A burning and a shining light
    To a' this place.

3

What was I, or my generation,
such That I should get sic† exaltation?
I, wha deserv'd most just damnation
    For broken laws
Six Sax† thousand years ere my creation,
    Thro' Adam's cause!

4

When from my mither's womb I fell,
Thou might hae plung'd me deep in hell
gums To gnash my gooms,† and weep, and wail
    In burning lakes,
Whare damnèd devils roar and yell,
    Chain'd to their stakes.

5

Yet I am here, a chosen sample,
To show Thy grace is great and ample:
I'm here a pillar o' Thy temple,
    Strong as a rock,
A guide, a buckler, and example
    To a' Thy flock!

6

But yet, O Lord! confess I must:
At times I'm fash'd⁺wi' fleshly lust;   irked
An' sometimes, too, in warldly trust,
    Vile self gets in;
But Thou remembers we are dust,
    Defiled wi' sin.

7

O Lord! yestreen,⁺ Thou kens,⁺ wi' Meg – last night;
Thy pardon I sincerely beg –   knowest
O, may't ne'er be a living plague
    To my dishonor!
An' I'll ne'er lift a lawless leg
    Again upon her.

8

Besides, I farther maun⁺avow –   must
Wi' Leezie's lass, three times, I trow –
But, Lord, that Friday I was fou,⁺   drunk
    When I cam near her,
Or else, Thou kens, Thy servant true
    Wad⁺never steer⁺her.   would; meddle with

9

Maybe Thou lets this fleshly thorn
Buffet Thy servant e'en and morn,
Lest he owre⁺proud and high should turn too
    That he's sae gifted:
If sae, Thy han' maun e'en be borne
    Until Thou lift it.

10

Lord, bless Thy chosen in this place,
For here Thou has a chosen race!
But God confound their stubborn face
    An' blast their name,
Wha bring Thy elders to disgrace
    An' open shame!

11

Lord, mind Gau'n Hamilton's deserts:
He drinks, an' swears, an' plays at cartes,⁺ cards
Yet has sae monie takin arts
    Wi' great and sma',
Frae God's ain Priest the people's hearts
    He steals awa.

12

And when we chasten'd him therefore,

row Thou kens how he bred sic a splore,[†]

And set the warld in a roar

O' laughin at us:

Curse Thou his basket and his store,

Kail an' potatoes!

13

Lord, hear my earnest cry and pray'r

Against that Presbyt'ry of Ayr!

Thy strong right hand, Lord, mak it bare

Upo' their heads!

do not Lord, visit them, an' dinna[†]spare,

For their misdeeds!

14

O Lord, my God! that glib-tongu'd Aiken,

My vera heart and flesh are quakin

To think how we stood sweatin, shakin,

pissed An' pish'd[†]wi' dread,

sneering While he, wi' hingin lip an' snakin,[†]

Held up his head.

15

Lord, in Thy day o' vengeance try him!

Lord, visit him wha did employ him!

And pass not in Thy mercy by them,

Nor hear their pray'r,

But for Thy people's sake destroy them,

An' dinna spare!

16

But, Lord, remember me and mine

Wi' mercies temporal and divine,

wealth That I for grace an' gear[†]may shine

Excell'd by nane;

And a' the glory shall be Thine –

Amen, Amen!

[106]

A POET'S WELCOME TO HIS BASTART WEAN[†]

little one

THE FIRST INSTANCE THAT ENTITLED HIM TO THE VENERABLE APPELLATION OF FATHER

1

Thou's welcome, wean! Mishanter fa'[†]me,
If thoughts o' thee or yet thy mammie
Shall ever daunton me or awe me,
  My sweet, wee lady,
Or if I blush when thou shalt ca' me
  Tyta or daddie!

Mishap befall

2

What tho' they ca' me fornicator,
An' tease my name in kintra clatter?[†]
The mair they talk, I'm kend the better;
  E'en let them clash![†]
An auld wife's tongue's a feckless[†]matter
  To gie ane fash.[†]

country gossip

tattle

feeble

give one annoyance

3

Welcome, my bonie, sweet, wee dochter!
Tho' ye come here a wee unsought for,
And tho' your comin I hae fought for
  Baith kirk and queir;
Yet, by my faith, ye're no unwrought for –
  That I shall swear!

4

Sweet fruit o' monie a merry dint,
My funny toil is no a' tint:[†]
Tho' thou cam to the warl' asklent,[†]
  Which fools may scoff at,
In my last plack[†]thy part's be in't
  The better half o't.

not all lost

askew

farthing

5

Tho' I should be the waur bestead,[†]
Thou's be as braw[†]and bienly[†]clad,
And thy young years as nicely bred
  Wi' education,
As onie brat o' wedlock's bed
  In a' thy station.

worse provided

finely; comfortably

6

Wee image o' my bonie Betty,
pet   As fatherly I kiss and daut[†]thee,
As dear and near my heart I set thee.
Wi' as guid will,
As a' the priests had seen me get thee
That's out o' Hell.

7

God   Gude[†]grant that thou may ay inherit
Thy mither's looks an' gracefu' merit,
An' thy poor, worthless daddie's spirit
Without his failins!
'Twill please me mair to see thee heir it
farms   Than stocket mailins.[†]

8

And if thou be what I wad hae thee,
An' tak the counsel I shall gie thee,
I'll never rue my trouble wi' thee –
The cost nor shame o't –
But be a loving father to thee,
And brag the name o't.

TO THE GUIDWIFE OF
WAUCHOPE HOUSE

(MRS SCOTT)

1

Guid Wife,
remember   I mind[†]it weel, in early date,
bashful   When I was beardless, young, and blate,[†]
An' first could thresh the barn,
hold; a day's work   Or haud[†]a yokin[†]at the pleugh,
exhausted   An', tho' forfoughten[†]sair eneugh,

Yet unco†proud to learn;   *mighty*
When first amang the yellow corn
  A man I reckon'd was,
An' wi' the lave ilk†merry morn   *others each*
  Could rank my rig†and lass: *ridge*
    Still shearing,† and clearing   *reaping*
      The tither stookèd raw,†   *row of shocks*
    Wi' clavers†an' havers†   *gossip; nonsense*
      Wearing the day awa.†   *away*

2

E'en then, a wish (I mind its pow'r),
A wish that to my latest hour
  Shall strongly heave my breast,
That I for poor auld Scotland's sake
Some usefu' plan or book could make,
  Or sing a sang at least.
The rough burr-thistle spreading wide
  Amang the bearded bear,†   *barley*
I turn'd the weeder-clips†aside,   *-shears*
  An' spar'd the symbol dear.
    No nation, no station
      My envy e'er could raise;
    A Scot still, but†blot still,   *without*
      I knew nae higher praise.

3

But still the elements o' sang
In formless jumble, right an' wrang,
  Wild floated in my brain;
Till on that hairst†I said†before,   *harvest; mentioned*
My partner in the merry core,†   *band*
  She rous'd the forming strain.
I see her yet, the sonsie quean†   *pleasant lass*
  That lighted up my jingle,
Her witching smile, her pauky een†   *artful eyes*
  That gart†my heart-strings tingle! *made*
    I firèd, inspirèd,
      At ev'ry kindling keek,†   *glance*
    But, bashing†and dashing,†   *abashed;*
      I fearèd ay to speak.   *put to shame*

4

Hale†to the sex! (ilk†guid chiel†says): *Health; each;*
Wi' merry dance on winter days,   *fellow*

An' we to share in common!
The gust o' joy, the balm of woe,
soul   The saul[†]o' life, the heav'n below
Is rapture-giving Woman.
churls   Ye surly sumphs,[†] who hate the name,
Be mindfu' o' your mither:
She, honest woman, may think shame
That ye're connected with her!
sad   Ye're wae[†]men, ye're nae men
That slight the lovely dears;
To shame ye, disclaim ye,
fellow   Ilk honest birkie[†]swears.

5

not; cowhouse   For you, no[†]bred to barn and byre,[†]
Wha sweetly tune the Scottish lyre,
Thanks to you for your line!
special   The marl'd[†]plaid ye kindly spare,
worn   By me should gratefully be ware;[†]
perfection   'Twad please me to the nine.[†]
proud; wrap   I'd be mair vauntie[†]o' my hap,[†]
sedately hanging;
rump   Douce hingin[†]owre my curple,[†]
folded   Than onie ermine ever lap,[†]
Or proud imperial purple.
long health   Farewell, then! lang hale,[†] then,
lot   An' plenty be your fa'![†]
May losses and crosses
porch   Ne'er at your hallan[†]ca'!

R. BURNS

March 1787

[110]

ADDRESS OF BEELZEBUB

To the Right Honorable the Earl of Breadalbane, President
of the Right Honorable the Highland Society, which met on
the 23rd of May last, at the *Shakespeare*, Covent Garden, to
concert ways and means to frustrate the designs of five hundred
Highlanders who, as the Society were informed by Mr.
M'Kenzie of Applecross, were so audacious as to attempt an
escape from their lawful lords and masters whose property
they were, by emigrating from the lands of Mr. Macdonald of
Glengary to the wilds of Canada, in search of that
fantastic thing – Liberty.

Long life, my lord, an' health be yours,
Unskaith'd† by hunger'd Highland boors!   Unharmed
Lord grant nae duddie,† desperate beggar,   ragged
Wi' dirk, claymore, or rusty trigger,
May twin† auld Scotland o' a life   rob
She likes – as lambkins like a knife!

Faith! you and Applecross were right
To keep the Highland hounds in sight!
I doubt na! they wad bid† nae better   offer
Than let them ance out owre the water!
Then up amang thae† lakes and seas,   those
They'll mak what rules and laws they please:
Some daring Hancock, or a Franklin,
May set their Highland bluid a-ranklin;
Some Washington again may head them,
Or some Montgomerie, fearless, lead them;
Till (God knows what may be effected
When by such heads and hearts directed)
Poor dunghill sons of dirt an' mire
May to Patrician rights aspire!
Nae sage North now, nor sager Sackville,
To watch and premier owre the pack vile!
An' whare will ye get Howes and Clintons
To bring them to a right repentance?
To cowe† the rebel generation,   scare
An' save the honor o' the nation?
They, an' be damn'd! what right hae they
To meat or sleep or light o' day,

Far less to riches, pow'r, or freedom,
But what your lordship likes to gie them?

But hear, my lord! Glengary, hear!
too Your hand's owre†light on them, I fear:
Your factors, grieves, trustees, and bailies,
gaily I canna say but they do gaylies:†
They lay aside a' tender mercies,
strip; slovens; bristles An' tirl†the hullions†to the birses.†
distrained; robbed Yet while they're only poind†and herriet,†
They'll keep their stubborn Highland spirit.
chips But smash them! crush them a' to spails,†
bankrupts An' rot the dyvors†i' the jails!
The young dogs, swinge them to the labor:
Let wark an' hunger mak them sober!
girls; at all good-looking The hizzies,† if they're aughtlins fawsont,†
Let them in Drury Lane be lesson'd!
An' if the wives an' dirty brats
begging; gates flapping with rags; vermin Come thiggin†at your doors an' yetts,†
Flaffin wi' duds†an' grey wi' beas',†
ducks Frightin awa your deuks†an' geese,
bulldog Get out a horsewhip or a jowler,†
The langest thong, the fiercest growler,
make An' gar†the tatter'd gypsies pack
Wi' a' their bastards on their back!

long Go on, my Lord! I lang†to meet you,
An' in my 'house at hame' to greet you.
shall not Wi' common lords ye shanna†mingle:
inmost corner; fireside The benmost neuk†beside the ingle,†
At my right han' assigned your seat
'Tween Herod's hip an' Polycrate,
weary Or (if you on your station tarrow†)
Between Almagro and Pizarro,
A seat, I'm sure ye're weel deservin't;
An' till ye come – your humble servant,

BEELZEBUB

HELL,
1st June, Anno Mundi 5790

PART TWO

SONGS

SONG

TUNE: *Corn Rigs*

1

It was upon a Lammas night,
   When corn rigs†are bonie,   ridges
Beneath the moon's unclouded light,
   I held awa to Annie;
The time flew by, wi' tentless†heed;   careless
   Till, 'tween the late and early,†   dark and
Wi' sma' persuasion she agreed   dawn
   To see me thro' the barley.
         Corn rigs, an' barley rigs,
            An' corn rigs are bonie:
            I'll ne'er forget that happy night,
              Amang the rigs wi' Annie.

2

The sky was blue, the wind was still,
   The moon was shining clearly;
I set her down, wi' right good will,
   Amang the rigs o' barley:
I ken't†her heart was a' my ain;   knew
   I lov'd her most sincerely;
I kiss'd her owre and owre again,
   Amang the rigs o' barley.

3

I lock'd her in my fond embrace;
   Her heart was beating rarely:
My blessings on that happy place,
   Amang the rigs o' barley!
But by the moon and stars so bright,
   That shone that hour so clearly!
She ay shall bless that happy night
   Amang the rigs o' barley.

4

I hae been blythe wi' comrades dear;
I hae been merry drinking;
money-
making
I hae been joyfu' gath'rin gear;[†]
I hae been happy thinking:
But a' the pleasures e'er I saw,
  Tho' three times doubl'd fairly –
That happy night was worth them a',
  Amang the rigs o' barley.
    Corn rigs, an' barley rigs,
      An' corn rigs are bonie:
      I'll ne'er forget that happy night,
      Amang the rigs wi' Annie.

rushes

GREEN GROW THE RASHES,[†] O

CHORUS

Green grow the rashes, O;
Green grow the rashes, O;
The sweetest hours that e'er I spend,
Are spent among the lasses, O.

1

There's nought but care on ev'ry han',
  In every hour that passes, O:
What signifies the life o' man,
  An' 'twere na for the lasses, O.

2

worldly
The war'ly[†]race may riches chase,
  An' riches still may fly them, O;
An' tho' at last they catch them fast,
  Their hearts can ne'er enjoy them, O.

3

quiet
But gie me a cannie[†]hour at e'en,
  My arms about my dearie, O,

An' war'ly†cares an' war'ly men   worldly
    May a' gae tapsalteerie,† O!   topsy-turvy

4

For you sae douce,† ye sneer at this;   sedate
    Ye're nought but senseless asses, O:
The wisest man the warl'†e'er saw,   world
    He dearly lov'd the lasses, O.

5

Auld Nature swears, the lovely dears
    Her noblest work she classes, O:
Her prentice han' she try'd on man,
    An' then she made the lasses, O.

CHORUS

Green grow the rashes, O ;
Green grow the rashes, O ;
The sweetest hours that e'er I spend
Are spent among the lasses, O.

M'PHERSON'S FAREWELL

CHORUS

Sae rantingly,† sae wantonly,   jovially
    Sae dauntingly gaed†he,   went
He play'd a spring, and danc'd it round
    Below the gallows-tree.

1

Farewell, ye dungeons dark and strong,
    The wretch's destinie!
M'Pherson's time will not be long
    On yonder gallows-tree.

2

O, what is death but parting breath?
    On many a bloody plain
I've dar'd his face, and in this place
    I scorn him yet again!

3

Untie these bands from off my hands,
    And bring to me my sword,
And there's no a man in all Scotland
    But I'll brave him at a word.

4

trouble

I've liv'd a life of sturt†and strife;
   I die by treacherie:
It burns my heart I must depart,
   And not avengèd be.

5

Now farewell light, thou sunshine bright,
   And all beneath the sky!
May coward shame distain his name,
   The wretch that dare not die!

CHORUS
Sae rantingly, sae wantonly,
   Sae dauntingly gaed he,
He play'd a spring, and danc'd it round
   Below the gallows-tree.

I'M O'ER YOUNG TO MARRY YET

CHORUS
I'm o'er young, I'm o'er young,
   I'm o'er young to marry yet!
I'm o'er young, 'twad be a sin
   To tak me frae my mammie yet.

1

only child
strange

I fear

I am my mammie's ae bairn,†
   Wi' unco†folk I weary, Sir,
And lying in a man's bed,
   I'm fley'd†it make me eerie, Sir.

2

one

Hallowmass is come and gane,
   The nights are lang in winter, Sir,
And you an' I in ae†bed –
   In trowth, I dare na venture, Sir!

3

woods

way
older be by

Fu' loud and shrill the frosty wind
   Blaws thro' the leafless timmer,† Sir,
But if ye come this gate†again,
   I'll aulder be gin†simmer, Sir.

CHORUS
I'm o'er young, I'm o'er young,
   I'm o'er young to marry yet!
I'm o'er young, 'twad be a sin
   To tak me frae my mammie yet.

O, WHISTLE AN' I'LL COME TO YE,
MY LAD

CHORUS

O, whistle an' I'll come to ye, my lad!
O, whistle an' I'll come to ye, my lad!
Tho' father an' mother an' a' should gae†mad,   go
O, whistle an' I'll come to ye, my lad!

1

But warily tent†when ye come to court me,   spy
And come nae†unless the back-yett†be a-jee;†   not; -gate; ajar
Syne†up the back-style, and let naebody see,   Then
And come as ye were na†comin to me,   not
And come as ye were na comin to me!

2

At kirk, or at market, whene'er ye meet me,
Gang†by me as tho' that ye car'd na a flie;†   Go; fly
But steal me a blink†o' your bonie black e'e,   glance
Yet look as ye were na lookin to me,
Yet look as ye were na lookin to me!

3

Ay vow and protest that ye care na for me,
And whyles†ye may lightly†my beauty a wee;†   sometimes; disparage; little
But court na anither tho' jokin ye be,
For fear that she wyle†your fancy frae me,   entice
For fear that she wyle your fancy frae me!

CHORUS

O, whistle an' I'll come to ye, my lad!
O, whistle an' I'll come to ye, my lad!
Tho' father an' mother an' a' should gae mad,
O, whistle an' I'll come to ye, my lad!

MY HIGHLAND LASSIE, O

CHORUS

Within the glen sae bushy, O,
Above; *Aboon*[†] *the plain sae rashy,*[†] *O,*
rushy *I set me down wi' right guid will*
To sing my Highland lassie, O!

1

No highborn   Nae gentle[†] dames, tho' ne'er sae fair,
Shall ever be my Muse's care:
Their titles a' are empty show –
Give   Gie[†] me my Highland lassie, O!

2

O, were yon hills and vallies mine,
Yon palace and yon gardens fine,
The world then the love should know
I bear my Highland lassie, O!

3

But fickle Fortune frowns on me,
must   And I maun[†] cross the raging sea;
But while my crimson currents flow
I'll love my Highland lassie, O.

4

Altho' thro' foreign climes I range,
I know her heart will never change;
For her bosom burns with honor's glow,
My faithful Highland lassie, O.

5

For her I'll dare the billows' roar,
For her I'll trace a distant shore,
That Indian wealth may lustre throw
Around my Highland lassie, O.

[120]

She has my heart, she has my hand,
My secret troth and honor's band!
'Till the mortal stroke shall lay me low,
I'm thine, my Highland lassie, O!

CHORUS

Farewell the glen sae bushy, O!
Farewell the plain sae rashy, O!
To other lands I now must go
To sing my Highland lassie, O.

DUNCAN GRAY

1

Weary fa'†you, Duncan Gray! Woe befall
 (Ha, ha, the girdin†o't!) girthing
Wae gae by†you, Duncan Gray Woe go with
 (Ha, ha, the girdin o't!)
When a' the lave†gae to their play, rest
Then I maun†sit the lee-lang†day, must; live-long
And jeeg†the cradle wi' my tae,† jog; toe
 And a' for the girdin o't!

2

Bonie was the Lammas moon
 (Ha, ha, the girdin o't!)
Glowrin†a' the hills aboon† Glaring; above
 (Ha, ha, the girdin o't!).
The girdin brak, the beast cam down,
I tint my curch†and baith my shoon,† kerchief; shoes
And, Duncan, ye're an unco loun†– terrible rogue
 Wae on the bad girdin o't!

[121]

3

if; oath   But Duncan, gin[†]ye'll keep your aith[†]
           (Ha, ha, the girdin o't!),
I'll   I'se[†]bless you wi' my hindmost breath
           (Ha, ha, the girdin o't!).
           Duncan, gin ye'll keep your aith,
           The beast again can bear us baith,
Minister; damage   And auld Mess[†]John will mend the skaith[†]
patch   And clout[†]the bad girdin o't.

O'ER THE WATER TO CHARLIE

CHORUS

We'll o'er the water, we'll o'er the sea,
We'll o'er the water to Charlie!
Come weal, come woe, we'll gather and go,
And live and die wi' Charlie!

1

Come boat me o'er, come row me o'er
   Come boat me o'er to Charlie!
penny   I'll gie John Ross another bawbee[†]
   To boat me o'er to Charlie.

2

I lo'e weel my Charlie's name,
   Tho' some there be abhor him;
going   But O, to see Auld Nick gaun[†]hame,
   And Charlie's faes before him!

3

I swear and vow by moon and stars
   And sun that shines so early,
If I had twenty thousand lives,
   I'd die as aft for Charlie!

CHORUS

We'll o'er the water, we'll o'er the sea,
We'll o'er the water to Charlie!
Come weal, come woe, we'll gather and go,
And live and die wi' Charlie!

A ROSE-BUD,
BY MY EARLY WALK

1

A rose-bud, by my early walk
Adown a corn-inclosèd bawk,[†]   field-path
Sae gently bent its thorny stalk,
    All on a dewy morning.
Ere twice the shades o' dawn are fled,
In a' its crimson glory spread
And drooping rich the dewy head,
    It scents the early morning.

2

Within the bush her covert nest
A little linnet fondly prest,
The dew sat chilly on her breast,
    Sae early in the morning.
She soon shall see her tender brood,
The pride, the pleasure o' the wood,
Amang the fresh green leaves bedew'd,
    Awake the early morning.

3

So thou, dear bird, young Jeany fair,
On trembling string or vocal air
Shall sweetly pay the tender care
    That tents[†]thy early morning!   guards
So thou, sweet rose-bud, young and gay,
Shalt beauteous blaze upon the day,
And bless the parent's evening ray
    That watch'd thy early morning!

AND I'LL KISS THEE YET

CHORUS

And I'll kiss thee yet, yet,
And I'll kiss thee o'er again,
And I'll kiss thee yet, yet,
My bonie Peggy Alison.

1

When in my arms, wi' a' thy charms,
I clasp my countless treasure, O,
I seek nae mair o' Heav'n to share

such   Than sic†a moment's pleasure, O!

2

eyes   And by thy een†sae bonie blue
I swear I'm thine for ever, O!
And on thy lips I seal my vow,
And break it shall I never, O!

CHORUS

And I'll kiss thee yet, yet,
And I'll kiss thee o'er again,
And I'll kiss thee yet, yet,
My bonie Peggy Alison.

conquer

TO DAUNTON† ME

CHORUS

To daunton me, to daunton me,
An auld man shall never daunton me!

1

The blude-red rose at Yule may blaw,
The simmer lilies bloom in snaw,
The frost may freeze the deepest sea,
But an auld man shall never daunton me.

2

To daunton me, and me sae young,
Wi' his fause heart and flatt'ring tongue
That is the thing you ne'er shall see,
For an auld man shall never daunton me.

3

malt   For a' his meal and a' his maut,†
For a' his fresh beef and his saut,

For a' his gold and white monie,
An auld man shall never daunton me.

4

His gear⁺may buy him kye⁺and yowes,⁺   money; kine; sheep
His gear may buy him glens and knowes;⁺   knolls
But me he shall not buy nor fee,⁺   hire
For an auld man shall never daunton me.

5

He hirples twa-fauld⁺as he dow,⁺   hobbles two-fold; can
Wi' his teethless gab⁺and his auld beld pow,⁺ mouth; bald pate
And the rain rains down frae his red blear'd e'e –
That auld man shall never daunton me!

CHORUS

To daunton me, to daunton me,
An auld man shall never daunton me!

AY WAUKIN,⁺ O   ever awake

CHORUS

Ay waukin, O,
Waukin still and weary:
Sleep I can get nane
For thinking on my dearie.

1

Simmer's a pleasant time:
   Flowers of every color,
The water rins owre the heugh,⁺   crag
   And I long for my true lover.

2

When I sleep I dream,
   When I wauk I'm eerie,⁺   apprehensive
Sleep I can get nane
   For thinkin on my dearie.

[125]

3

rest

> Lanely night comes on,
> A' the lave†are sleepin,
> I think on my bonie lad,
> And I bleer my een†wi' greetin.†

eyes;
weeping

CHORUS

> *Ay waukin, O,*
> *Waukin still and weary:*
> *Sleep I can get nane*
> *For thinking on my dearie.*

cup

THE SILVER TASSIE†

1

> Go, fetch to me a pint o' wine,
> And fill it in a silver tassie,
> That I may drink before I go
> A service to my bonie lassie!
> The boat rocks at the pier o' Leith,
> Fu' loud the wind blaws frae the Ferry,
> The ship rides by the Berwick-Law,
> And I maun†leave my bonie Mary.

must

2

> The trumpets sound, the banners fly,
> The glittering spears are rankèd ready,
> The shouts o' war are heard afar,
> The battle closes deep and bloody.
> It's not the roar o' sea or shore
> Wad mak me langer wish to tarry,
> Nor shouts o' war that's heard afar:
> It's leaving thee, my bonie Mary!

rest of it

WHISTLE O'ER THE LAVE O'T†

1

> First when Maggie was my care,
> Heav'n, I thought, was in her air;
> Now we're married, spier nae mair,†
> But – whistle o'er the lave o't!

ask no more

Meg was meek, and Meg was mild,
Sweet and harmless as a child:
Wiser men than me's beguiled –
    Whistle o'er the lave o't!

2

How we live, my Meg and me,
How we love, and how we gree,[†]   agree
I care na[†]by how few may see –   care nothing
    Whistle o'er the lave o't!
Wha I wish were maggots' meat,
Dish'd up in her winding-sheet,
I could write (but Meg wad see't) –
Whistle o'er the lave o't!

RATTLIN, ROARIN WILLIE

1

O, rattlin, roarin Willie,
   O, he held to the fair,
An' for to sell his fiddle
   And buy some other ware;
But parting wi' his fiddle,
   The saut tear blin't his e'e –
And, rattlin, roarin Willie,
   Ye're welcome hame to me.

2

'O Willie, come sell your fiddle,
   O, sell your fiddle sae fine!
O Willie come sell your fiddle
   And buy a pint o' wine!'
'If I should sell my fiddle,
   The warld would think I was mad;
For monie a rantin[†]day   merry
   My fiddle and I hae had.'

[127]

3

quietly
looked in

board-end

As I cam by Crochallan,
   I cannily keekit ben,[†]
Rattlin, roarin Willie
   Was sitting at yon boord-en':[†]
Sitting at yon boord-en',
   And amang guid companie!
Rattlin, roarin Willie,
   Ye're welcome hame to me.

O TIBBIE, I HAE SEEN THE DAY

CHORUS

would not have
lack of wealth;
scorn
I care not although
you do

O Tibbie, I hae seen the day,
   Ye wadna[†]been sae shy!
For laik o' gear[†]ye lightly[†]me,
   But, trowth, I care na by.[†]

1

Last night
spoke not; went;
blowing dust
toss your head

devil a bit

Yestreen[†]I met you on the moor,
Ye spak na,[†] but gaed[†]by like stoure![†]
Ye geck[†]at me because I'm poor –
   But fient a hair[†]care I!

2

gave

cared

When comin hame on Sunday last,
Upon the road as I cam past,
Ye snufft an' gae[†]your head a cast –
   But, trowth, I care't[†]na by!

3

wealth

I doubt na, lass, but ye may think,
Because ye hae the name o' clink,[†]
That ye can please me at a wink,
   Whene'er ye like to try.

4

But sorrow tak him that's sae mean,
Altho' his pouch o' coin were clean,
Wha follows onie saucy quean,
   That looks sae proud and high!

5

Altho' a lad were e'er sae smart,
If that he want the yellow dirt,

Ye'll cast your head anither airt,[†]   *direction*
   And answer him fu' dry.

6

But if he hae the name o' gear,
Ye'll fasten to him like a brier,
Tho' hardly he for sense or lear[†]   *learning*
   Be better than the kye.[†]   *kine*

7

But, Tibbie, lass, tak my advice:
Your daddie's gear maks you sae nice,
The Deil a ane wad spier[†]your price,   *ask*
   Were ye as poor as I.

8

There lives a lass beside yon park,
I'd rather hae her in her sark[†]   *shift*
Than you wi' a' your thousand mark,
   That gars[†]you look sae high.   *makes*

CHORUS
O Tibbie, I hae seen the day,
   Ye wadna been sae shy!
For laik o' gear ye lightly me,
   But, trowth, I care na by.

MY HEART'S IN THE HIGHLANDS

CHORUS
My heart's in the Highlands, my heart is not here,
My heart's in the Highlands a-chasing the deer,
A-chasing the wild deer and following the roe –
My heart's in the Highlands, wherever I go!

1

Farewell to the Highlands, farewell to the North,
The birthplace of valor, the country of worth!
Wherever I wander, wherever I rove,
The hills of the Highlands for ever I love.

2

Farewell to the mountains high cover'd with
   snow,
Farewell to the straths and green valleys below,
Farewell to the forests and wild-hanging woods,
Farewell to the torrents and loud-pouring floods!

CHORUS

My heart's in the Highlands, my heart is not here,
My heart's in the Highlands a-chasing the deer,
A-chasing the wild deer and following the roe —
My heart's in the Highlands, wherever I go!

love

JOHN ANDERSON MY JO[†]

1

John Anderson my jo, John,

acquainted

  When we were first acquent,[†]
Your locks were like the raven,

straight
bald

  Your bonie brow was brent;[†]
But now your brow is beld,[†] John,
  Your locks are like the snaw,

pate

But blessings on your frosty pow,[†]
  John Anderson my jo!

2

John Anderson my jo, John,

climbed;
together

  We clamb[†] the hill thegither,[†]

jolly

And monie a cantie[†] day, John,
  We've had wi' ane anither;

must

Now we maun[†] totter down, John,
  And hand in hand we'll go,
And sleep thegither at the foot,
  John Anderson my jo!

OF A' THE AIRTS[†]

directions

1

Of a' the airts the wind can blaw
  I dearly like the west,
For there the bonie lassie lives,
  The lassie I lo'e best.
There wild woods grow, and rivers row,[†]   roll
  And monie a hill between,
But day and night my fancy's flight
  Is ever wi' my Jean.

2

I see her in the dewy flowers –
  I see her sweet and fair.
I hear her in the tunefu' birds –
  I hear her charm the air.
There's not a bonie flower that springs
  By fountain, shaw,[†] or green,   wood
There's not a bonie bird that sings,
  But minds[†]me o' my Jean.   reminds

MY LOVE, SHE'S BUT A LASSIE YET

CHORUS

My love, she's but a lassie yet,
My love, she's but a lassie yet!
We'll let her stand a year or twa,
She'll no be half sae saucy yet!

1

I rue the day I sought her, O!
I rue the day I sought her, O!
Wha gets her need na say he's woo'd,
  But he may say he has bought her, O.

2

Come draw a drap o' the best o't yet,
Come draw a drap o' the best o't yet!
^{Go} Gae†seek for pleasure whare ye will,
But here I never missed it yet.

3

We're a' dry wi' drinkin o't,
We're a' dry wi' drinkin o't!
The minister kiss't the fiddler's wife –
He could na preach for thinkin o't!

CHORUS

My love, she's but a lassie yet,
My love, she's but a lassie yet!
We'll let her stand a year or twa,
She'll no be half sae saucy yet!

Drive the
ewes to
the knolls

CA' THE YOWES TO THE KNOWES†

CHORUS

Ca' the yowes to the knowes,
Ca' them where the heather grows,
brooklet rolls *Ca' them where the burnie rowes,†*
My bonie dearie!

1

went As I gaed†down the water-side,
There I met my shepherd lad:
wrapped He row'd†me sweetly in his plaid,
called And he ca'd†me his dearie.

[132]

2

'Will ye gang†down the water-side,   go
And see the waves sae sweetly glide
Beneath the hazels spreading wide?
 The moon it shines fu' clearly.'

3

'I was bred up in nae sic†school,   such
My shepherd lad, to play the fool,
An' a' the day to sit in dool,†   sorrow
 An' naebody to see me.'

4

'Ye sall†get gowns and ribbons meet, shall
Cauf-†leather shoon upon your feet, Calf-
And in my arms thou'lt lie and sleep,
 An' ye sall be my dearie.'

5

'If ye'll but stand to what ye've said,
I'se gang†wi' you, my shepherd lad, I'll go
And ye may row me in your plaid,
 And I sall be your dearie.'

6

'While waters wimple†to the sea,   wind
While day blinks†in the lift†sae hie,† shines;
Till clay-cauld death sall blin' my e'e,   sky; high
 Ye sall be my dearie.'

CHORUS

Ca' the yowes to the knowes,
Ca' them where the heather grows,
Ca' them where the burnie rowes,
 My bonie dearie!

THOU LINGERING STAR

1

Thou ling'ring star with less'ning ray,
 That lov'st to greet the early morn,
Again thou usher'st in the day
 My Mary from my soul was torn.
O Mary, dear departed shade!
 Where is thy place of blissful rest?
See'st thou thy lover lowly laid?
 Hear'st thou the groans that rend his breast?

2

That sacred hour can I forget,
　　Can I forget the hallow'd grove,
Where, by the winding Ayr, we met
　　To live one day of parting love?
Eternity cannot efface
　　Those records dear of transports past,
Thy image at our last embrace –
　　Ah! little thought we 'twas our last!

3

Ayr, gurgling, kiss'd his pebbled shore,
　　O'erhung with wild woods thickening green;
The fragrant birch and hawthorn hoar
　　'Twin'd amorous round the raptur'd scene;
The flowers sprang wanton to be prest,
　　The birds sang love on every spray,
Till too, too soon, the glowing west
　　Proclaim'd the speed of wingèd day.

4

Still o'er these scenes my mem'ry wakes,
　　And fondly broods with miser-care.
Time but th' impression stronger makes,
　　As streams their channels deeper wear.
O Mary, dear departed shade!
　　Where is thy place of blissful rest?
See'st thou thy lover lowly laid?
　　Hear'st thou the groans that rend his breast?

rollicking　　　**THE RANTIN† DOG, THE DADDIE O'T**

1

-clothes　　　　O, wha my babie-clouts† will buy?
attend to　　　　O, wha will tent† me when I cry?
　　　　　　　Wha will kiss me where I lie? –
　　　　　　　　The rantin dog, the daddie o't!

2

fault　　　　　O, wha will own he did the faut?†
child-bed ale　　O' wha will buy the groanin maut?†
name it　　　　O' wha will tell me how to ca't?†–
　　　　　　　　The rantin dog, the daddie o't!

3

When I mount the creepie-chair,
Wha will sit beside me there?
Gie me Rob, I'll seek nae mair –
    The rantin dog, the daddie o't!

4

Wha will crack†to me my lane?†   talk; alone
Wha will mak me fidgin fain?†   tingling with
Wha will kiss me o'er again? –   eagerness
    The rantin dog, the daddie o't!

THE BATTLE OF SHERRAMUIR

1

'O, cam ye here the fight to shun,
    Or herd the sheep wi' me, man?
Or were ye at the Sherra-moor,
    Or did the battle see, man?'
'I saw the battle, sair and teugh,†   sore and tough
And reekin-red ran monie a sheugh;†   furrow
My heart for fear gae sough†for sough,   gave sigh
To hear the thuds, and see the cluds†   clouds
O' clans frae woods in tartan duds,†   clothes
    Wha glaum'd†at kingdoms three, man.   grasped

2

'The red-coat lads wi' black cockauds
    To meet them were na slaw,† man: not slow
They rush'd and push'd and bluid outgush'd,
    And monie a bouk†did fa', man!   trunk
The great Argyle led on his files,
I wat†they glanc'd†for twenty miles;   wot; shone
They hough'd†the clans like nine-pin kyles,† hocked; skittles
They hack'd and hash'd, while braid-swords
      clash'd,
And thro' they dash'd, and hew'd and smash'd,
    Till fey†men died awa, man.   fated

3

'But had ye seen the philibegs†   kilts
    And skyrin†tartan trews,† man,   flaring; trousers
When in the teeth they daur'd†our Whigs dared
    And Covenant trueblues, man!
In lines extended lang and large,

bayonets

When baig'nets†o'erpower'd the targe,
And thousands hasten'd to the charge,
Wi' Highland wrath they frae the sheath
Drew blades o' death, till out o' breath

pigeons

    They fled like frighted dows,† man!'

4

how the Devil

'O, how Deil!†Tam, can that be true?

went

    The chase gaed†frae the north, man!
I saw mysel, they did pursue
    The horseman back to Forth, man;
And at Dunblane, in my ain sight,

bridge

They took the brig†wi' a' their might,
And straught to Stirling wing'd their flight;
But, cursed lot! the gates were shut,
And monie a huntit poor red-coat,

almost;
  swoon

    For fear amaist†did swarf,† man!'

5

road

'My sister Kate cam up the gate†

meal and
      water

    Wi' crowdie†unto me, man:
She swoor she saw some rebels run
    To Perth and to Dundee, man!
Their left-hand general had nae skill:
The Angus lads had nae good will
That day their neebors' bluid to spill;
For fear by foes that they should lose

mugs of
  porridge

Their cogs o' brose,† they scar'd at blows,
    And hameward fast did flee, man.

6

'They've lost some gallant gentlemen,
    Amang the Highland clans, man!
I fear my Lord Panmure is slain,
    Or in his en'mies' hands, man.
Now wad ye sing this double flight,
Some fell for wrang, and some for right,
But monie bade the world guid-night:
Say, pell and mell, wi' muskets' knell
How Tories fell, and Whigs to Hell
    Flew off in frighted bands, man!'

WILLIE BREW'D A PECK O' MAUT[†] malt

CHORUS

We are na fou,[†] we're nae that fou, full (*i.e.* drunk)
 But just a drappie[†] in our e'e! droplet
The cock may craw,[†] the day may daw,[†] crow; dawn
 And ay we'll taste the barley-bree![†] -brew

1

O, Willie brew'd a peck o' maut,
 And Rob and Allan cam to see.
Three blyther hearts the lee-lang[†] night live-long
 Ye wad na[†] found in Christendie.[†] would not have;
            Christendom

2

Here are we met three merry boys,
 Three merry boys I trow are we;
And monie a night we've merry been,
 And monie mae[†] we hope to be! more

3

It is the moon, I ken her horn,
 That's blinkin[†] in the lift[†] sae hie:[†] shining; sky; high
She shines sae bright to wyle[†] us hame, entice
 But, by my sooth, she'll wait a wee!

4

Wha first shall rise to gang[†] awa, go
 A cuckold, coward loun[†] is he! rogue
Wha first beside his chair shall fa',
 He is the King amang us three!

CHORUS

We are na fou, we're nae that fou,
 But just a drappie in our e'e!
The cock may craw, the day may daw,
 And ay we'll taste the barley-bree!

TAM GLEN

1

My heart is a-breaking, dear tittie,†
    Some counsel unto me come len'
To anger them a' is a pity,
    But what will I do wi' Tam Glen?

2

such; fine
poverty;
  shift

must not

I'm thinking, wi' sic†a braw†fellow,
    In poortith†I might mak a fen'.†
What care I in riches to wallow,
    If I mauna†marry Tam Glen?

3

in

money

There's Lowrie the laird o' Dumeller:
    'Guid day to you,' brute! he comes ben.†
He brags and he blaws o' his siller,†
    But when will he dance like Tam Glen?

4

mother;
  deafen

My minnie†does constantly deave†me,
    And bids me beware o' young men.
They flatter, she says, to deceive me –
    But wha can think sae o' Tam Glen?

5

if

My daddie says, gin†I'll forsake him,
    He'd gie me guid hunder marks ten.
But if it's ordain'd I maun take him,
    O, wha will I get but Tam Glen?

6

Last night

mouth;
  bound

Yestreen†at the valentines' dealing,
    My heart to my mou†gied a sten,†
For thrice I drew ane without failing,
    And thrice it was written 'Tam Glen'!

7

wetted shift

stalking

breeches

The last Halloween I was waukin
    My droukit sark-sleeve,† as ye ken –
His likeness came up the house staukin,†
    And the very grey breeks†o' Tam Glen!

8

If

Come, counsel, dear tittie, don't tarry!
    I'll gie ye my bonie black hen,
Gif†ye will advise me to marry
    The lad I lo'e dearly, Tam Glen.

O JOHN, COME KISS ME NOW

CHORUS

O John, come kiss me now, now, now!
O John, my love, come kiss me now!
O John, come kiss me by and by,
For weel ye ken the way to woo!

1

O, some will court and compliment,
   And ither†some will kiss and daut;†   others; pet
But I will mak o' my guidman,†   husband
   My ain guidman – it is nae faut!†   fault

2

O, some will court and compliment,
   And ither some will prie†their mou',   taste
And some will hause†in ither's arms,   cuddle
   And that's the way I like to do!

CHORUS

O John, come kiss me now, now, now!
O John, my love, come kiss me now!
O John, come kiss me by and by,
For weel ye ken the way to woo!

CRAIGIEBURN WOOD

CHORUS

Beyond thee, dearie, beyond thee, dearie,
And O, to be lying beyond thee!
O, sweetly, soundly, weel may he sleep
That's laid in the bed beyond thee!

1

Sweet closes the ev'ning on Craigieburn Wood
   And blythely awaukens the morrow;
But the pride o' the spring on the Craigieburn
   Wood
   Can yield me naught but sorrow.

2

I see the spreading leaves and flowers,
   I hear the wild birds singing;
But pleasure they hae nane for me,
   While care my heart is wringing.

3

must

I can na tell, I maun'na tell,
    I daur na for your anger;
But secret love will break my heart,
    If I conceal it langer.

4

I see thee gracefu', straight, and tall,
    I see thee sweet and bonie;
But O, what will my torment be,
    If thou refuse thy Johnie!

5

To see thee in another's arms
    In love to lie and languish,

death

'Twad be my dead,† that will be seen –
    My heart wad burst wi' anguish!

6

But, Jeanie, say thou wilt be mine,
    Say thou lo'es nane before me,
And a' my days o' life to come
    I'll gratefully adore thee.

CHORUS

Beyond thee, dearie, beyond thee, dearie,
    And O, to be lying beyond thee!
O, sweetly, soundly, weel may he sleep
    That's laid in the bed beyond thee!

COCK UP YOUR BEAVER

1

When first my brave Johnie lad came to this
    town,
He had a blue bonnet that wanted the crown,
But now he has gotten a hat and a feather –
Hey, brave Johnie lad, cock up your beaver!

2

spruce

Cock up your beaver, and cock it fu' sprush!†
We'll over the border and gie them a brush:
There's somebody there we'll teach better
    behavior –
Hey, brave Johnie lad, cock up your beaver!

AE† FOND KISS
One

1

Ae fond kiss, and then we sever!
Ae farewell, and then forever!
Deep in heart-wrung tears I'll pledge thee,
Warring sighs and groans I'll wage thee.
Who shall say that Fortune grieves him,
While the star of hope she leaves him?
Me, nae cheerfu' twinkle lights me,
Dark despair around benights me.

2

I'll ne'er blame my partial fancy:
Naething could resist my Nancy!
But to see her was to love her,
Love but her, and love for ever.
Had we never lov'd sae kindly,
Had we never lov'd sae blindly,
Never met – or never parted –
We had ne'er been broken-hearted.

3

Fare-thee-weel, thou first and fairest!
Fare-thee-weel, thou best and dearest!
Thine be ilka†joy and treasure,   every
Peace, Enjoyment, Love and Pleasure!
Ae fond kiss, and then we sever!
Ae farewell, alas, for ever!
Deep in heart-wrung tears I'll pledge thee,
Warring sighs and groans I'll wage thee.

KILLIECRANKIE

CHORUS

If   *An⁺ye had been whare I hae been,*

would not   *Ye wad na⁺been sae cantie,⁺ O!*
    have; jolly

                   An ye had seen what I hae seen

heights   *On the braes⁺o' Killiecrankie, O!*

1

fine   'Whare hae ye been sae braw,⁺ lad?

spruce   Whare hae ye been sae brankie,⁺ O?

                   Whare hae ye been sae braw, lad?

                     Cam ye by Killiecrankie, O?'

2

'I faught at land, I faught at sea,

      At hame I faught my auntie, O;

But I met the Devil and Dundee

      On the braes o' Killiecrankie, O.

3

furrow   'The bauld Pitcur fell in a furr,⁺

knock   An' Clavers gat a clankie,⁺ O,

Else; hawk   Or⁺I had fed an Athole gled⁺

                    On the braes o' Killiecrankie, O!'

CHORUS

An ye had been whare I hae been,

      Ye wad na been sae cantie, O!

An ye had seen what I hae seen

      On the braes o' Killiecrankie, O!

WHA IS THAT AT MY BOWER DOOR?

1

'Wha is that at my bower door?'

      'O, wha is it but Findlay!'

go your way; ye shall not   'Then gae your gate,⁺ ye'se nae⁺be here.'

must   'Indeed maun⁺I!' quo' Findlay.

do   'What mak⁺ye, sae like a thief?'

                     'O, come and see!' quo' Findlay.

'Before the morn ye'll work mischief?'

                     'Indeed will I!' quo' Findlay.

'Gif†I rise and let you in' –   If
    'Let me in!' quo' Findlay –
'Ye'll keep me wauken†wi' your din?'   awake
    'Indeed will I!' quo' Findlay.
'In my bower if ye should stay' –
    'Let me stay!' quo' Findlay –
'I fear ye'll bide till break o' day?'
    'Indeed will I!' quo' Findlay.

'Here this night if ye remain' –
    'I'll remain!' quo' Findlay –
'I dread ye'll learn the gate again?'
    'Indeed will I!' quo' Findlay.
'What may pass within this bower'
    ('Let it pass!' quo' Findlay!)
'Ye maun conceal till your last hour' –
    'Indeed will I!' quo' Findlay.

BONIE WEE THING

CHORUS

Bonie wee thing, cannie†wee thing,   gentle
    Lovely wee thing, wert thou mine,
I wad wear thee in my bosom
    Lest my jewel it should tine.†   lose

1

Wishfully I look and languish
    In that bonie face o' thine,
And my heart it stounds†wi' anguish,   aches
    Lest my wee thing be na mine.

2

Wit and Grace and Love and Beauty
    In ae†constellation shine!   one
To adore thee is my duty,
    Goddess o' this soul o' mine!

CHORUS

Bonie wee thing, cannie wee thing,
    Lovely wee thing, wert thou mine,
I wad wear thee in my bosom
    Lest my jewel it should tine.

KELLYBURN BRAES

1

<small>old man</small>   There lived a carl⁺in Kellyburn Braes
     (Hey and the rue grows bonie wi' thyme!),
And he had a wife was the plague o' his days
     (And the thyme it is wither'd, and rue is in
         prime!).

2

<small>One</small>   Ae⁺day as the carl gaed up the lang glen
     (Hey and the rue grows bonie wi' thyme!),
<small>are you
  getting on</small> He met wi' the Devil, says: – 'How do you fen?'⁺
     (And the thyme it is wither'd, and rue is in
         prime!).

3

'I've got a bad wife, sir, that's a' my complaint
     (Hey and the rue grows bonie wi thyme!),
For, saving your presence, to her ye're a saint'
     (And the thyme it is wither'd, and rue is in
         prime!).

4

<small>steer; young
   horse</small> 'It's neither your stot⁺nor your staig⁺I shall crave
     (Hey and the rue grows bonie wi' thyme!),
'But gie me your wife, man, for her I must have'
     (And the thyme it is wither'd, and rue is in
         prime!).

5

'O welcome most kindly!' the blythe carl said
     (Hey and the rue grows bonie wi' thyme!),
<small>worse</small>   'But if ye can match her ye're waur⁺than ye're ca'd'
     (And the thyme it is wither'd, and rue is in
         prime!).

6

The Devil has got the auld wife on his back
  (Hey and the rue grows bonie wi' thyme!),
And like a poor pedlar he's carried his pack
  (And the thyme it is wither'd, and rue is in
     prime!).

7

He's carried her hame to his ain hallan†-door   porch-
  (Hey and the rue grows bonie wi' thyme!),
Syne†bade her gae†in for a bitch and a whore   Then; go
  (And the thyme it is wither'd, and rue is in
     prime!).

8

Then straight he makes fifty, the pick o' his band
  (Hey and the rue grows bonie wi' thyme!),
Turn out on her guard in the clap o' a hand
  (And the thyme it is wither'd, and rue is in
     prime!).

9

The carlin†gaed thro' them like onie wud†bear   beldam; mad
  (Hey and the rue grows bonie wi' thyme!):
Whae'er she gat hands on cam ne'er her nae mair
  (And the thyme it is wither'd, and rue is in
     prime!).

10

A reekit wee†deevil looks over the wa   smoky small
  (Hey and the rue grows bonie wi' thyme!): –
'O help, maister, help, or she'll ruin us a'!'
  (And the thyme it is wither'd, and rue is in
     prime!).

11

The Devil he swore by the edge o' his knife
  (Hey and the rue grows bonie wi' thyme!),
He pitied the man that was tied to a wife
  (And the thyme it is wither'd, and rue is in
     prime!).

12

The Devil he swore by the kirk and the bell
  (Hey and the rue grows bonie wi' thyme!),
He was not in wedlock, thank Heav'n, but in Hell
  (And the thyme it is wither'd, and rue is in
     prime!).

[145]

13

Then Satan has travell'd again wi' his pack
  (Hey and the rue grows bonie wi' thyme!),
And to her auld husband he's carried her back
  (And the thyme it is wither'd, and rue is in
    prime!).

14

most   'I hae been a Devil the feck†o' my life
  (Hey and the rue grows bonie wi' thyme!),
But ne'er was in Hell till I met wi' a wife'
  (And the thyme it is wither'd, and rue is in
    prime!).

One-   # O, FOR ANE†-AND-TWENTY, TAM

CHORUS

An' O, for ane-and-twenty, Tam!
  And hey, sweet ane-and-twenty, Tam!
I'll learn my kin a rattlin sang
If   *An†I saw ane-and-twenty, Tam.*

1

snub; sore; keep   They snool†me sair,† and haud†me down,
make; a stupid   And gar†me look like bluntie,† Tam;
But three short years will soon wheel roun' –
  And then comes ane-and-twenty, Tam!

2

A patch of land; A gleib o' lan',† a claut o' gear†
handful of money   Was left me by my auntie, Tam.
Of; ask   At†kith or kin I needna spier,†
  An I saw ane-and-twenty, Tam.

3

dolt   They'll hae me wed a wealthy coof,†
  Tho' I mysel hae plenty, Tam;
palm   But hear'st thou, laddie – there's my loof:†
  I'm thine at ane-and-twenty, Tam!

CHORUS

An' O, for ane-and-twenty, Tam!
  And hey, sweet ane-and-twenty, Tam!
I'll learn my kin a rattlin sang
  An I saw ane-and-twenty, Tam.

SWEET AFTON

1

Flow gently, sweet Afton, among thy green
    braes![†]   slopes
Flow gently, I'll sing thee a song in thy praise!
My Mary's asleep by thy murmuring stream –
Flow gently, sweet Afton, disturb not her dream!

2

Thou stock dove whose echo resounds thro' the
    glen,
Ye wild whistling blackbirds in yon thorny den,
Thou green-crested lapwing, thy screaming
    forbear –
I charge you, disturb not my slumbering fair!

3

How lofty, sweet Afton, thy neighboring hills,
Far mark'd with the courses of clear, winding
    rills!
There daily I wander, as noon rises high,
My flocks and my Mary's sweet cot in my eye.

4

How pleasant thy banks and green vallies below,
Where wild in the woodlands the primroses blow
There oft, as mild Ev'ning weeps over the lea,
The sweet-scented birk[†]shades my Mary and me. birch

5

Thy crystal stream, Afton, how lovely it glides,
And winds by the cot where my Mary resides!
How wanton thy waters her snowy feet lave,
As, gathering sweet flowerets, she stems thy clear
    wave!

6

Flow gently, sweet Afton, among thy green braes!
Flow gently, sweet river, the theme of my lays!
My Mary's asleep by thy murmuring stream –
Flow gently, sweet Afton, disturb not her dream!

IT WAS
A' FOR OUR RIGHTFU' KING

1

It was a' for our rightfu' king
  We left fair Scotland's strand;
It was a' for our rightfu' king,
  We e'er saw Irish land,
    My dear –
  We e'er saw Irish land.

2

Now a' is done that men can do,
  And a' is done in vain,
My Love and Native Land fareweel,
  For I maun†cross the main,
    My dear –
  For I maun cross the main.

must

3

He turn'd him right and round about
  Upon the Irish shore,
And gae†his bridle reins a shake,
  With adieu for evermore,
    My dear –
  And adieu for evermore!

gave

4

The soger frae the wars returns,
  The sailor frae the main,
But I hae parted frae my love
  Never to meet again,
    My dear –
  Never to meet again.

5

When day is gane, and night is come,
  And a' folk bound to sleep,
I think on him that's far awa
  The lee-lang†night, and weep,
    My dear –
  The lee-lang night and weep.

live-long

THE DEIL'S AWA WI' TH'
EXCISEMAN

CHORUS

The Deil's awa, the Deil's awa,
  The Deil's awa wi' th' Exciseman!
He's danc'd awa, he's danc'd awa,
  He's danc'd awa wi' th' Exciseman!

1

The Deil cam fiddlin thro' the town,
  And danc'd awa wi' th' Exciseman,
And ilka⁺wife cries: – 'Auld Mahoun,⁺   every; Satan
  I wish you luck o' the prize, man!

2

'We'll mak our maut,⁺and we'll brew our drink, malt
  We'll laugh, sing, and rejoice, man,
And monie braw⁺thanks to the meikle⁺black   handsome;
  Deil,   big
  That danc'd awa wi' th' Exciseman.

3

There's threesome reels, there's foursome reels,
  There's hornpipes and strathspeys, man,
But the ae⁺best dance ere cam to the land   one
  Was *The Deil's Awa wi th' Exciseman.*

CHORUS

The Deil's awa, the Deil's awa,
  The Deil's awa wi' th' Exciseman!
He's danc'd awa, he's danc'd awa,
  He's danc'd awa wi' th' Exciseman!

HERE'S HIS HEALTH IN WATER

Altho' my back be at the wa',⁺   wall
  And tho' he be the fautor,⁺   transgressor
Altho' my back be at the wa',
  Yet here's his health in water!
O, wae gae⁺by his wanton sides,   woe go
  Sae brawly's⁺he could flatter!   finely as
Till for his sake I'm slighted sair
  And dree the kintra clatter!⁺   endure the
But, tho' my back be at the wa',   talk of the
  Yet here's his health in water!   countryside

[149]

WILT THOU BE MY DEARIE?

1

Wilt thou be my dearie?
When Sorrow wrings thy gentle heart,
   O, wilt thou let me cheer thee?
By the treasure of my soul –
   That's the love I bear thee –
I swear and vow that only thou
   Shall ever be my dearie!
Only thou, I swear and vow,
   Shall ever be my dearie!

2

Lassie, say thou lo'es me,
Or, if thou wilt na be my ain,†   *own*
   Say na thou'lt refuse me!
If it winna,† canna be,   *will not*
   Thou for thine may choose me,
Let me, lassie, quickly die,
   Trusting that you lo'es me!
Lassie, let me quickly die,
   Trusting that thou lo'es me!

O, AN† YE WERE DEAD, GUIDMAN†

if; husband

CHORUS

Sing, round about the fire wi' a rung† she ran,   *cudgel*
An' round about the fire wi' a rung she ran : –
'Your horns shall tie you to the staw,†   *stall*
An' I shall bang your hide, guidman!'

1

O, an ye were dead, guidman,
A green turf on your head, guidman!
I wad bestow my widowhood
Upon a rantin† Highlandman!   *roistering*

There's sax†eggs in the pan, guidman,   six
There's sax eggs in the pan, guidman:
There's ane to you, and twa to me,
And three to our John Highlandman!

3

A sheep-head's in the pot, guidman,
A sheep-head's in the pot, guidman:
The flesh to him, the broo†to me,   broth
An' the horns become your brow, guidman!

CHORUS

Sing, round about the fire wi' a rung she ran,
An' round about the fire wi' a rung she ran: –
'Your horns shall tie you to the staw,
An' I shall bang your hide, guidman!'

AULD LANG SYNE†   Old long ago

CHORUS

For auld lang syne, my dear,
For auld lang syne,
We'll tak a cup o' kindness yet
For auld lang syne!

1

Should auld acquaintance be forgot,
   And never brought to mind?
Should auld acquaintance be forgot,
   And auld lang syne!

2

And surely ye'll be†your pint-stowp,   pay for
   And surely I'll be mine,
And we'll tak a cup o' kindness yet
   For auld lang syne!

3

We twa hae run about the braes,†   hillsides
   And pou'd†the gowans†fine,   pulled; wild daisies
But we've wander'd monie a weary fit†   foot
   Sin'†auld lang syne.   Since

4

We twa hae paidl'd†in the burn†   waded; brook
   Frae morning sun till dine,†   noon

broad	But seas between us braid[†]hae roar'd
	Sin' auld lang syne.

5

chum	And there's a hand, my trusty fiere,[†]
give me	And gie's[†]a hand o' thine,
hearty toast	And we'll tak a right guid-willie waught[†]
	For auld lang syne!

CHORUS

For auld lang syne, my dear,
For auld lang syne,
We'll tak a cup o' kindness yet
For auld lang syne!

reaped; harvest

ROBIN SHURE[†] IN HAIRST[†]

CHORUS

Robin shure in hairst,
I shure wi' him:

Devil; sickle   *Fient[†]a heuk[†]had I,*

stuck   *Yet I stack[†]by him.*

1

went	I gaed[†]up to Dunse
web of coarse woollen	To warp a wab o' plaiden[†]
gate	At his daddie's yett[†]
	Wha met me but Robin!

2

Wasn't; bold	Was na[†]Robin bauld,[†]
cottager	Tho' I was a cottar?[†]
such	Play'd me sic[†]a trick,
Elder's daughter	An' me the Eller's dochter![†]

3

Robin promis'd me

food	A' my winter vittle:[†]
Fiend have it (*i.e.* Nothing)	Fient haet[†]he had but three
Goose-quills; knife	Guse feathers[†]and a whittle![†]

CHORUS

Robin shure in hairst,
I shure wi' him:
Fient a heuk had I,
Yet I stack by him.

A RED, RED ROSE

1

O, my luve is like a red, red rose,
    That's newly sprung in June.
O, my luve is like the melodie,
    That's sweetly play'd in tune.

2

As fair art thou, my bonie lass,
    So deep in luve am I,
And I will luve thee still, my dear,
    Till a' the seas gang[†]dry.   go

3

Till a' the seas gang dry, my dear,
    And the rocks melt wi' the sun!
And I will luve thee still, my dear,
    While the sands o' life shall run.

4

And fare thee weel, my only luve,
    And fare thee weel a while!
And I will come again, my luve,
    Tho' it were ten thousand mile!

HAD I THE WYTE?[†]

Was I to
    blame?

1

Had I the wyte? had I the wyte?
    Had I the wyte? she bade me!
She watch'd me by the hie-gate[†]side,   highway
    And up the loan[†]she shaw'd[†]me;   lane; showed
And when I wadna[†]venture in,   would not
    A coward loon[†]she ca'd me!   rascal
Had Kirk and State been in the gate,[†]   there to
    I'd lighted when she bade me.   oppose

2

led me in	Sae craftilie she took me ben[†]
noise	And bade me mak nae clatter[†]: –
surly husband	'For our ramgunshoch, glum guidman[†]
beyond	Is o'er ayont[†]the water.'
	Whae'er shall say I wanted grace,
fondle	When I did kiss and dawte[†]her,
	Let him be planted in my place,
Then; transgressor	Syne[†]say I was the fautor![†]

3

	Could I for shame, could I for shame,
have refused	Could I for shame refus'd[†]her?
would not; have been	And wadna[†]manhood been[†]to blame
	Had I unkindly used her?
wool-comb	He claw'd her wi' the ripplin-kame,[†]
blue	And blae[†]and bluidy bruis'd her –
such	When sic[†]a husband was frae hame,
would have	What wife but wad[†]excus'd her!

4

wiped; eyes	I dighted[†]ay her een[†]sae blue,
cursed; scoundrel	An' bann'd[†]the cruel randy,[†]
wot; mouth	And, weel I wat,[†] her willin mou'[†]
	Was sweet as sugarcandie.
sunset	At gloamin-shot,[†] it was, I wot,
	I lighted – on the Monday,
Tuesday's	But I cam thro' the Tyseday's[†]dew
	To wanton Willie's brandy.

COMIN THRO' THE RYE

CHORUS

wet; creature	*O, Jenny's a' weet,[†] poor body,[†]*
	Jenny's seldom dry:
draggled	*She draigl't[†]a' her petticoatie,*
	Comin thro' the rye!

1

Comin thro' the rye, poor body,
Comin thro' the rye,
She draigl't a' her petticoatie,
Comin thro' the rye!

2

Should	Gin[†]a body meet a body
	Comin thro' the rye,

Gin a body kiss a body,
   Need a body cry?

3

Gin a body meet a body
   Comin thro' the glen,
Gin a body kiss a body,
   Need the warld ken?

CHORUS

O, Jenny's a' weet, poor body,
   Jenny's seldom dry:
She draigl't a' her petticoatie,
   Comin thro' the rye!

FOR THE SAKE O' SOMEBODY

1

My heart is sair†– I dare na tell –   sore
   My heart is sair for Somebody:
I could wake a winter night
   For the sake o' Somebody.
     O-hon! for Somebody!
     O-hey! for Somebody!
I could range the world around
   For the sake o' Somebody.

2

Ye Powers that smile on virtuous love,
   O, sweetly smile on Somebody!
Frae ilka†danger keep him free,   each
   And send me safe my Somebody!
     O-hon! for Somebody!
     O-hey! for Somebody!
I wad do – what wad I not? –
   For the sake o' Somebody!

CHARLIE HE'S MY DARLING

An' Charlie he's my darling,
My darling, my darling,
Charlie he's my darling –
The Young Chevalier!

1

'Twas on a Monday morning
    Right early in the year,
That Charlie came to our town –
    The Young Chevalier!

2

As he was walking up the street
    The city for to view,
O, there he spied a bonie lass
    The window looking thro'!

3

Sae light's he jimpèd up the stair,
    And tirl'd at the pin;†
And wha sae ready as hersel'
    To let the laddie in!

scratched at
the door

4

He set his Jenny on his knee,
    All in his Highland dress;
For brawlie weel†he kend the way
    To please a bonie lass.

finely well

5

It's up yon heathery mountain
    And down yon scroggy†glen,

scrubby

[156]

We daurna gang[†]a-milking   daren't go
    For Charlie and his men!

CHORUS

An' Charlie he's my darling,
My darling, my darling,
Charlie he's my darling –
The Young Chevalier!

I'LL AY CA' IN BY YON TOWN

CHORUS

I'll ay ca'[†]in by yon town   call
   And by yon garden green again!
I'll ay ca' in by yon town,
   And see my bonie Jean again.

1

There's nane shall ken, there's nane can guess
   What brings me back the gate again,[†]   same way
But she, my fairest faithfu' lass,
   And stow'nlins[†]we sall meet again.   by stealth

2

She'll wander by the aiken[†]tree,   oaken
   When trystin[†]time draws near again;   meeting
And when her lovely form I see,
   O haith![†] she's doubly dear again.   faith

CHORUS

I'll ay ca' in by yon town
   And by yon garden green again!
I'll ay ca' in by yon town,
   And see my bonie Jean again.

WE'RE A' NODDIN

CHORUS

We're a' noddin,
Nid nid noddin,
We're a' noddin
At our house at hame!

1

gossip   'Guid e'en to you, kimmer,[†]
     And how do ye do?'
'Hiccup!' quo' kimmer,
drunk   'The better that I'm fou!'[†]

2

corner   Kate sits i' the neuk,[†]
chicken-   Suppin hen-broo.[†]
    broth   Deil tak Kate
     An she be na noddin too!

3

How are all   'How's a'[†]wi' you, kimmer?
     And how do you fare?'
'A pint o' the best o't,
     And twa pints mair!'

4

'How's a' wi' you, kimmer?
     And how do ye thrive?
How monie bairns hae ye?'
     Quo' kimmer, 'I hae five.'

5

'Are they a' Johnie's?'
in truth   'Eh! atweel[†]na:
Twa o' them were gotten
     When Johnie was awa!'

6

Cats like milk,
broth   And dogs like broo;[†]
Lads like lasses weel,
     And lasses lads too.

CHORUS

We're a' noddin,
Nid nid noddin,
We're a' noddin
At our house at hame!

THE HIGHLAND WIDOW'S
LAMENT

1

O, I am come to the low countrie –
  Ochon, ochon, ochrie! –
Without a penny in my purse
  To buy a meal to me.

2

It was na sae†in the Highland hills –   not so
  Ochon, ochon, ochrie! –
Nae woman in the country wide
  Sae happy was as me.

3

For then I had a score o' kye†–   kine
  Ochon, ochon, ochrie! –
Feeding on yon hill sae high
  And giving milk to me.

4

And there I had three score o' yowes†–   ewes
  Ochon, ochon, ochrie! –
Skipping on yon bonie knowes†   knolls
  And casting woo'†to me.   wool

5

I was the happiest of a' the clan –
  Sair,† sair may I repine! –   sorely
For Donald was the brawest man,†   pick of the
  And Donald he was mine.   clan

6

Till Charlie Stewart cam at last
  Sae far to set us free:
My Donald's arm was wanted then
  For Scotland and for me.

7

woeful

Their waefu'†fate what need I tell?
Right to the wrang did yield:
My Donald and his country fell
Upon Culloden field.

8

Ochon! O Donald, O!
Ochon, ochon, ochrie!
Nae woman in the warld wide
Sae wretched now as me!

hand

O, LAY THY LOOF† IN MINE, LASS

CHORUS

O, lay thy loof in mine, lass,
In mine, lass, in mine, lass,
And swear on thy white hand, lass,

own

That thou wilt be my ain!†

1

often; much
woe
foe

A slave to Love's unbounded sway,
He aft†has wrought me meikle wae;†
But now he is my deadly fae,†
Unless thou be my ain.

2

moment

There's monie a lass has broke my rest,
That for a blink†I hae lo'ed best;
But thou art queen within my breast,
For ever to remain.

CHORUS

O, lay thy loof in mine, lass,
In mine, lass, in mine, lass,
And swear on thy white hand, lass,
That thou wilt be my ain!

O, STEER† HER UP, AN' HAUD HER GAUN†

rouse; keep her going

1

O, steer her up, an' haud her gaun –
  Her mither's at the mill, jo,
An' gin†she winna†tak a man,   *if; will not*
  E'en let her tak her will, jo.
First shore†her wi' a gentle kiss,   *threaten*
  And ca'†anither gill, jo,   *call for*
An' gin†she tak the thing amiss,   *should she*
  E'en let her flyte†her fill, jo.   *scold*

2

O, steer her up, an' be na blate,†   *not bashful*
  An' gin she tak it ill, jo,
Then leave the lassie till†her fate,   *to*
  And time nae langer spill,† jo!   *waste*
Ne'er break your heart for ae rebute,† *one rebuff*
  But think upon it still, jo,
That gin the lassie winna do't,
  Ye'll fin'†anither will, jo.   *find*

LORD GREGORY

1

O, mirk,† mirk is this midnight hour,   *dark*
  And loud the tempest's roar!
A waefu' wanderer seeks thy tower –
  Lord Gregory, ope thy door.

2

An exile frae her father's ha',†   *hall*
  And a' for sake o' thee,
At least some pity on me shaw,†   *show*
  If love it may na be.

3

Lord Gregory mind'st†thou not the grove *rememb'rest*
  By bonie Irwine side,
Where first I own'd that virgin love
  I lang, lang had denied?

4

How aften didst thou pledge and vow,
  Thou wad for ay be mine!
And my fond heart, itsel' sae true,
  It ne'er mistrusted thine.

5

Hard is thy heart, Lord Gregory,
 And flinty is thy breast:
Thou bolt of Heaven that flashest by,
 O, wilt thou bring me rest!

6

Ye mustering thunders from above,
 Your willing victim see,
But spare and pardon my fause love
 His wrangs to Heaven and me!

THOU GLOOMY DECEMBER

1

Once more Ance mair†I hail thee, thou gloomy December!
 Ance mair I hail thee wi' sorrow and care!
Sad was the parting thou makes me remember:
 Parting wi' Nancy, O, ne'er to meet mair!

2

Fond lovers' parting is sweet, painful pleasure,
 Hope beaming mild on the soft parting hour;
But the dire feeling, O farewell for ever!
 Anguish unmingled and agony pure!

3

Wild as the winter now tearing the forest,
 Till the last leaf o' the summer is flown –
Such is the tempest has shaken my bosom,
 Till my last hope and last comfort is gone!

4

Still as I hail thee, thou gloomy December,
 Still shall I hail thee wi' sorrow and care;
For sad was the parting thou makes me
  remember:
 Parting wi' Nancy, O, ne'er to meet mair!

CONTENTED WI' LITTLE

1

jolly Contented wi' little and cantie†wi' mair,
 Whene'er I forgather wi' Sorrow and Care,
smack I gie them a skelp,† as they're creepin alang,
mug of new Wi' a cog o' guid swats†and an auld Scottish sang.
  ale

[162]

2

I whyles claw†the elbow o' troublesome Thought;   sometimes scratch
But Man is a soger, and Life is a faught.†   fight
My mirth and guid humor are coin in my pouch,
And my Freedom's my lairdship nae monarch
    daur touch.

3

A towmond†o' trouble, should that be my fa',†   twelvemonth; lot
A night o' guid fellowship sowthers†it a':   solders
When at the blythe end o' our journey at last,
Wha the Deil ever thinks o' the road he has past?

4

Blind Chance, let her snapper†and stoyte†on her   stumble; stagger
    way,
Be't to me, be't frae me, e'en let the jade gae!†   go
Come Ease or come Travail, come Pleasure or
    Pain,
My warst†word is: – 'Welcome, and welcome   worst
    again!'

O POORTITH CAULD†   cold poverty

CHORUS

O, why should Fate sic†pleasure have   such
   Life's dearest bands untwining?
Or why sae sweet a flower as love
   Depend on Fortune's shining?

1

O Poortith cauld and restless Love,
   Ye wrack†my peace between ye!   wreck
Yet poortith a' I could forgive,
   An†'twere na for my Jeanie.   If

2

The warld's wealth when I think on,
   Its pride and a' the lave†o't –   rest
My curse on silly coward man,
   That he should be the slave o't!

3

Her een†sae bonie blue betray   eyes
   How she repays my passion;
But prudence is her o'erword ay:
   She talks o' rank and fashion.

4

O, wha can prudence think upon,
  And sic a lassie by him?
O, wha can prudence think upon,
  And sae in love as I am?

5

How blest the wild-wood Indian's fate!
  He woos his artless dearie –
hobgoblins The silly bogles,† Wealth and State,
fearful   Can never make him eerie.†

CHORUS

O, why should Fate sic pleasure have,
  Life's dearest bands untwining?
Or why sae sweet a flower as love
  Depend on Fortune's shining?

Handsome ## BRAW† LADS O' GALLA WATER

1

heights Braw, braw lads on Yarrow braes,†
  They rove amang the blooming heather;
woods But Yarrow braes nor Ettrick shaws†
  Can match the lads o' Galla Water.

2

But there is ane, a secret ane,
Above   Aboon†them a' I loe him better;
And I'll be his, and he'll be mine,
  The bonie lad o' Galla Water.

3

land-owner Altho' his daddie was nae laird,†
much dowry   And tho' I hae nae meikle tocher,†
Yet, rich in kindest, truest love,
watch   We'll tent†our flocks by Galla Water.

[164]

It ne'er was wealth, it ne'er was wealth,
    That cott[†]contentment, peace, and pleasure: bought
The bands and bliss o' mutual love,
    O, that's the chiefest warld's treasure!

WANDERING WILLIE

1

Here awa, there awa, wandering Willie,
    Here awa, there awa, haud awa hame![†]   head for home
Come to my bosom, my ae[†]only dearie,   one
    And tell me thou bring'st me my Willie the
        same.

2

Loud tho' the Winter blew cauld at our parting,
    'Twas na the blast brought the tear in my e'e:
Welcome now Simmer,[†] and welcome my Willie,   Summer
    The Simmer to Nature, my Willie to me!

3

Rest, ye wild storms in the cave o' your
        slumbers –
    How your wild howling a lover alarms!
Wauken,[†] ye breezes, row[†]gently, ye billows,   Awake; roll
    And waft my dear laddie ance mair to my
        arms.

4

But O, if he's faithless, and minds na[†]his Nannie,   remembers not
    Flow still between us, thou wide-roaring main!
May I never see it, may I never trow it,
    But, dying, believe that my Willie's my ain!

SAW YE BONIE LESLEY

1

O, saw ye bonie Lesley,
    As she gaed[†]o'er the Border?   went
She's gane, like Alexander,
    To spread her conquests farther!

2

To see her is to love her,
    And love but her for ever;
For Nature made her what she is,
    And never made anither!

3

Thou art a queen, fair Lesley –
  Thy subjects, we before thee!
Thou art divine, fair Lesley –
  The hearts o' men adore thee.

4

harm

belong to

The Deil he could na skaith†thee,
  Or aught that wad belang†thee:
He'd look into thy bonie face,
  And say: – 'I canna wrang thee!'

5

above; guard

meddle with

The Powers aboon†will tent†thee,
  Misfortune sha'na steer†thee:
Thou'rt like themsel' sae lovely,
  That ill they'll ne'er let near thee.

6

Return again, fair Lesley,
  Return to Caledonie!
That we may brag we hae a lass
  There's nane again sae bonie.

THERE WAS A LASS

1

There was a lass, and she was fair!
  At kirk and market to be seen
When a' our fairest maids were met,
  The fairest maid was bonie Jean.

2

And ay she wrought her country wark,
  And ay she sang sae merrilie:
The blythest bird upon the bush
  Had ne'er a lighter heart than she!

3

linnet's

But hawks will rob the tender joys,
  That bless the little lintwhite's†nest,
And frost will blight the fairest flowers,
  And love will break the soundest rest.

4

handsomest

oxen; kine

horses

Young Robie was the brawest†lad,
  The flower and pride of a' the glen,
And he had owsen,† sheep, and kye,†
  And wanton naigies†nine or ten.

5

He gaed† wi' Jeanie to the tryste,   went
   He danc'd wi' Jeanie on the down,
And, lang ere witless Jeanie wist,
   Her heart was tint,† her peace was stown!†   lost; stolen

6

As in the bosom of the stream
   The moon-beam dwells at dewy e'en,
So, trembling pure, was tender love
   Within the breast of bonie Jean.

7

And now she works her country's wark,
   And ay she sighs wi' care and pain,
Yet wist na† what her ail† might be,   knew not; complaint
   Or what wad make her weel† again.   well

8

But did na† Jeanie's heart loup† light,   not; leap
   And did na joy blink† in her e'e,   glance
As Robie tauld a tale o' love
   Ae† e'enin on the lily lea?   One

9

While monie a bird sang sweet o' love,
   And monie a flower blooms o'er the dale,
His cheek to hers he aft did lay,
   And whisper'd thus his tender tale:

10

'O Jeanie fair, I lo'e thee dear
   O, canst thou think to fancy me?
Or wilt thou leave thy mammie's cot,
   And learn to tent† the farms wi' me?   tend

11

'At barn or byre† thou shalt na drudge,   cowhouse
   Or naething else to trouble thee,
But stray amang the heather-bells,
   And tent the waving corn wi' me.'

12

Now what could artless Jeanie do?
   She had nae will to say him na!
At length she blush'd a sweet consent,
   And love was ay between them twa.

LAST MAY A BRAW† WOOER

fine

1

Last May a braw wooer cam down the lang glen,
    And sair wi' his love he did deave†me.
I said there was naething I hated like men:
    The deuce gae†wi'm to believe me, believe me –
    The deuce gae wi'm to believe me!

2

He spak o' the darts in my bonie black een,†
    And vow'd for my love he was diein.
I said, he might die when he liket for Jean:
    The Lord forgie me for liein, for liein –
    The Lord forgie me for liein!

3

A weel-stocket mailen,† himsel for the laird,†
    And marriage aff-hand were his proffers:
I never loot†on that I kenn'd it, or car'd,
    But thought I might hae waur†offers, waur
      offers –
    But thought I might hae waur offers.

4

But what wad ye think? In a fortnight or less
    (The Deil tak his taste to gae near her!)
He up the Gate-Slack to my black cousin, Bess!
    Guess ye how, the jad!† I could bear her, could
      bear her –
    Guess ye how, the jad! I could bear her.

5

But a' the niest†week, as I petted†wi' care,
    I gaed to the tryste†o' Dalgarnock,

Glosses (left margin): fine · deafen · go · eyes · farm; landlord · let · worse · wanton · next; sulked · cattle-fair

And wha but my fine fickle lover was there?
   I glowr'd†as I'd seen a warlock, a warlock –   stared
   I glowr'd as I'd seen a warlock.

6

But owre my left shouther†I gae him a blink,†   shoulder;
   Lest neebours might say I was saucy.   glance
My wooer he caper'd as he'd been in drink,
   And vow'd I was his dear lassie, dear lassie –
   And vow'd I was his dear lassie!

7

I spier'd†for my cousin fu' couthy†and sweet: asked; affable
   Gin†she had recover'd her hearin?   If
And how her new shoon†fit her auld, shachl'd†   shoes;
    feet?   shapeless
   But heavens! how he fell a swearin, a swearin –
   But heavens! how he fell a swearin!

8

He beggèd, for gudesake,† I wad be his wife,   God's sake
   Or else I wad kill him wi' sorrow;
So e'en to preserve the poor body in life,
   I think I maun†wed him to-morrow,   must
    to-morrow –
   I think I maun wed him to-morrow!

SCOTS, WHA HAE†   who have

1

Scots, wha hae wi' Wallace bled,
Scots, wham Bruce has aften led,
Welcome to your gory bed
       Or to victorie!

2

Now's the day, and now's the hour
See the front o' battle lour,
See approach proud Edward's power –
       Chains and slaverie!

3

Wha will be a traitor knave?
Wha can fill a coward's grave?
Wha sae base as be a slave? –
    Let him turn, and flee!

4

Wha for Scotland's King and Law
Freedom's sword will strongly draw,
Freeman stand or freeman fa',
    Let him follow me!

5

By Oppression's woes and pains,
By your sons in servile chains,
We will drain our dearest veins
    But they shall be free!

6

Lay the proud usurpers low!
Tyrants fall in every foe!
Liberty's in every blow!
    Let us do, or die!

O, LET ME IN THIS AE† NIGHT

one

CHORUS

O, let me in this ae night,
This ae, ae, ae night!
O, let me in this ae night,
And rise, and let me in!

1

O lassie, are ye sleepin yet,
Or are ye waukin,† I wad wit?†
For Love has bound me hand an' fit,†
    And I would fain be in, jo.

awake!
know

foot

2

Thou hear'st the winter wind an' weet:†
Nae star blinks†thro' the driving sleet!
Tak pity on my weary feet,
    And shield me frae the rain, jo.

wet

shines

3

The bitter blast that round me blaws,
Unheeded howls, unheeded fa's:

The cauldness o' thy heart's the cause
  Of a' my care and pine, jo.

CHORUS

O, let me in this ae night,
This ae, ae, ae night!
O, let me in this ae night,
  And rise and let me in!

HER ANSWER

CHORUS

I tell you now this ae night
This ae, ae, ae night,
And ance for a' this ae night,
I winna†let ye in, jo.   will not

1

O, tell me na†o' wind an' rain,   not
Upbraid na me wi' cauld disdain,
Gae back the gate†ye cam again,   way
  I winna let ye in, jo!

2

The snellest†blast at mirkest†hours,   keenest;
That round the pathless wand'rer pours   darkest
Is nocht†to what poor she endures,   nothing
  That's trusted faithless man, jo.

3

The sweetest flower that deck'd the mead,
Now trodden like the vilest weed –
Let simple maid the lesson read!
  The weird†may be her ain,† jo.   fate; own

4

The bird that charm'd his summer day,
And now the cruel fowler's prey,
Let that to witless woman say : –
  'The gratefu' heart of man,' jo.

CHORUS

I tell you now this ae night,
This ae, ae, ae night,
And ance for a' this ae night,
I winna let ye in, jo.

CHORUS

O, this is no my ain lassie,
Fair tho' the lassie be:
Weel ken I my ain lassie –
eye   *Kind love is in her e'e.*†

1

I see a form, I see a face,
Ye weel may wi' the fairest place:
It wants to me the witching grace,
    The kind love that's in her e'e.

2

She's bonie, blooming, straight, and tall,
And lang has had my heart in thrall;
soul   And ay it charms my very saul,†
    The kind love that's in the e'e.

3

artful   A thief sae pawkie†is my Jean,
glance   To steal a blink†by a' unseen!
sharp   But gleg†as light are lover's een,
    When kind love is in the e'e.

4

It may escape the courtly sparks,
It may escape the learned clerks;
But well the watching lover marks
    The kind love that's in her e'e.

O, this is no my ain lassie,
Fair tho' the lassie be:
Weel ken I my ain lassie –
Kind love is in her e'e.

HIGHLAND MARY

1

Ye banks and braes and streams around
   The castle o' Montgomery,
Green be your woods, and fair your flowers,
   Your waters never drumlie!†   turbid
There Summer first unfald†her robes,   unfold
   And there the langest tarry!
For there I took the last fareweel
   O' my sweet Highland Mary!

2

How sweetly bloom'd the gay, green birk,†   birch
   How rich the hawthorn's blossom,
As underneath their fragrant shade
   I clasp'd her to my bosom!
The golden hours on angel wings
   Flew o'er me and my dearie:
For dear to me as light and life
   Was my sweet Highland Mary.

3

Wi' monie a vow and lock'd embrace
   Our parting was fu' tender;
And, pledging aft to meet again,
   We tore oursels asunder.
But O, fell Death's untimely frost,
   That nipt my flower sae early!
Now green's the sod, and cauld's the clay,
   That wraps my Highland Mary!

4

O, pale, pale now, those rosy lips
   I aft hae kiss'd sae fondly;
And clos'd for ay, the sparkling glance
   That dwalt on me sae kindly;

And mouldering now in silent dust
That heart that lo'ed me dearly!
But still within my bosom's core
Shall live my Highland Mary.

IS THERE FOR HONEST POVERTY

1

Is there for honest poverty
That hings†his head, an' a' that? *hangs*
The coward slave, we pass him by –
We dare be poor for a' that!
For a' that, an' a' that,
Our toils obscure, an' a' that,
The rank is but the guinea's stamp,
The man's the gowd†for a' that. *gold*

2

What though on hamely fare we dine,
Wear hoddin grey,† an' a' that? *coarse grey woollen*
Gie fools their silks, and knaves their wine –
A man's a man for a' that.
For a' that, an' a' that,
Their tinsel show, an' a' that,
The honest man, tho' e'er sae poor,
Is king o' men for a' that.

3

Ye see yon birkie ca'd† 'a lord,' *fellow called*
Wha struts, an' stares, an' a' that?
Tho' hundreds worship at his word,
He's but a cuif†for a' that. *dolt*
For a' that, an' a' that,
His ribband, star, an' a' that,
The man o' independent mind,
He looks an' laughs at a' that.

4

A prince can mak a belted knight,
A marquis, duke, an' a' that!
But an honest man's aboon†his might – *above*
Guid faith, he mauna fa'†that! *must not fail*
For a' that, an' a' that,
Their dignities, an' a' that,
The pith o' sense an' pride o' worth
Are higher rank than a' that.

Then let us pray that come it may
  (As come it will for a' that)
That Sense and Worth o'er a' the earth
  Shall bear the gree†an' a' that!   *have the first place*
For a' that, an' a' that,
  It's comin yet for a' that,
That man to man the world o'er
  Shall brithers be for a' that.

THERE WAS A LAD

CHORUS

Robin was a rovin boy,
   Rantin,† rovin, rantin, rovin,   *roistering*
Robin was a rovin boy,
   Rantin, rovin Robin!

1

There was a lad was born in Kyle,
But whatna†day o' whatna style,   *what*
I doubt it's hardly worth the while
  To be sae nice wi' Robin.

2

Our monarch's hindmost year but ane†   *one*
Was five-and-twenty days begun,
'Twas then a blast o' Janwar' win'†   *January wind*
  Blew hansel†in on Robin.   *the first gift*

3

The gossip keekit†in his loof,†   *glanced; palm*
Quo' scho:†– 'Wha lives will see the proof,   *Quoth she*
This waly†boy will be nae coof:†   *thumping; dolt*
  I think we'll ca' him Robin.

4

'He'll hae misfortunes great an' sma',
But ay a heart aboon†them a'.   *above*
He'll be a credit till†us a':   *to*
  We'll a' be proud o' Robin!

5

'But sure as three times three mak nine,
I see by ilka†score and line,   *every*
This chap will dearly like our kin',†   *kind*
  So leeze me on†thee, Robin!   *Commend me to*

6

sir　　　　　'Guid faith,' quo' scho, 'I doubt you, stir,†
make; aspread　Ye gar†the lasses lie aspar;†
faults; worse　But twenty fauts†ye may hae waur†–
　　　　　　　So blessins on thee, Robin!'

CHORUS

Robin was a rovin boy,
Rantin, rovin, rantin, rovin,
Robin was a rovin boy,
Rantin, rovin Robin!

meadow-ridge　　　　　THE LEA-RIG†

1

When o'er the hill the eastern star
folding　　　　Tells bughtin†time is near, my jo,
And owsen frae the furrow'd field
dull　　　　　Return sae dowf†and weary, O,
birches　　Down by the burn, where scented birks†
　　　Wi' dew are hangin clear, my jo,
I'll meet thee on the lea-rig,
　My ain kind dearie, O.

2

darkest　　At midnight hour in mirkest†glen
frightened　　I'd rove, and ne'er be eerie,† O,
went　　If thro' that glen I gaed†to thee,
　　My ain kind dearie, O!
Altho' the night were ne'er sae wild,
　And I were ne'er sae weary, O,
I'll meet thee on the lea-rig,
　My ain kind dearie, O.

3

The hunter lo'es the morning sun
　To rouse the mountain deer, my jo;
At noon the fisher takes the glen
　Adown the burn to steer, my jo:
twilight　Gie me the hour o' gloamin†grey –
　It maks my heart sae cheery, O,
To meet thee on the lea-rig,
　My ain kind dearie, O!

MARY MORISON

1

O Mary, at thy window be!
  It is the wish'd, the trysted hour.
Those smiles and glances let me see,
    That make the miser's treasure poor.
    How blythely wad I bide the stoure,[†]   bear the struggle
A weary slave frae sun to sun,
    Could I the rich reward secure –
The lovely Mary Morison!

2

Yestreen,[†] when to the trembling string   Last night
  The dance gaed[†]thro' the lighted ha',   went
To thee my fancy took its wing,
    I sat, but neither heard or saw:
    Tho' this was fair, and that was braw,[†]   fine
And yon[†]the toast of a' the town,   the other
    I sigh'd and said amang them a': –
'Ye are na Mary Morison!'

3

O Mary, canst thou wreck his peace
  Wha for thy sake wad gladly die?
Or canst thou break that heart of his
    Whase only faut[†]is loving thee?   fault
    If love for love thou wilt na gie,[†]   give
At least be pity to me shown:
    A thought ungentle canna[†]be   cannot
The thought o' Mary Morison.

MY FATHER WAS A FARMER

1

My father was a farmer upon the Carrick border,
  O,
And carefully he bred me in decency and order,
  O.
He bade me act a manly part, though I had ne'er
  a farthing, O,
For without an honest, manly heart no man was
  worth regarding, O.

2

Then out into the world my course I did
  determine, O:
Tho' to be rich was not my wish, yet to be great
  was charming, O.
My talents they were not the worst, nor yet my
  education, O –
Resolv'd was I at least to try to mend my
  situation, O.

3

In many a way and vain essay I courted
  Fortune's favor, O:
Some cause unseen still stept between to frustrate
  each endeavor, O.
Sometimes by foes I was o'erpower'd, sometimes
  by friends forsaken, O,
And when my hope was at the top, I still was
  worst mistaken, O.

4

Then sore harass'd, and tir'd at last with
  Fortune's vain delusion, O,
I dropt my schemes like idle dreams, and came to
  this conclusion, O: –
The past was bad, and the future hid; its good or
  ill untrièd, O,
But the present hour was in my pow'r, and so I
  would enjoy it, O.

5

No help, nor hope, nor view had I, nor person to
  befriend me, O;
So I must toil, and sweat, and broil, and labor
  to sustain me, O!

To plough and sow, to reap and mow, my father
    bred me early, O:
For one, he said, to labor bred was a match for
    Fortune fairly, O.

6

Thus all obscure, unknown, and poor, thro' life
    I'm doom'd to wander, O,
Till down my weary bones I lay in everlasting
    slumber, O.
No view nor care, but shun whate'er might breed
    me pain or sorrow, O,
I live to-day as well's I may, regardless of
    tomorrow, O!

7

But, cheerful still, I am as well as a monarch in a
    palace, O,
Tho' Fortune's frown still hunts me down, with
    all her wonted malice, O:
I make indeed my daily bread, but ne'er can
    make it farther, O,
But, as daily bread is all I need, I do not much
    regard her, O.

8

When sometimes by my labor I earn a little
    money, O,
Some unforeseen misfortune comes gen'rally
    upon me, O:
Mischance, mistake, or by neglect, or my good-
    natur'd folly, O –
But, come what will, I've sworn it still, I'll ne'er
    be melancholy, O.

9

All you who follow wealth and power with
    unremitting ardor, O,
The more in this you look for bliss, you leave
    your view the farther, O.
Had you the wealth Potosi boasts, or nations to
    adore you, O,
A cheerful, honest-hearted clown I will prefer
    before you, O!

SWEET ARE THE BANKS

1

Sweet are the banks, the banks o' Doon,
   The spreading flowers are fair,
And everything is blythe and glad,
   But I am fu' o' care.
Thou'll break my heart, thou bonie bird,
   That sings upon the bough!
reminds   Thou minds†me o' the happy days
   When my fause Luve was true.
Thou'll break my heart, thou bonie bird,
   That sings beside thy mate,
For sae I sat, and sae I sang,
   And wist na o' my fate!

2

Aft hae I rov'd by bonie Doon,
   To see the woodbine twine,
each   And ilka†bird sang o' its luve,
   And sae did I o' mine.
plucked   Wi' lightsome heart I pu'd†a rose
   Upon its thorny tree,
stole   But my fause luver staw†my rose,
   And left the thorn wi' me.
Wi' lightsome heart I pu'd a rose
   Upon a morn in June,
And sae I flourish'd on the morn,
before   And sae was pu'd or†noon.

LOGAN WATER

1

O Logan, sweetly didst thou glide
That day I was my Willie's bride,
since then And years sin syne hae†o'er us run
have   Like Logan to the simmer sun.
But now thy flowery banks appear
dull   Like drumlie†winter, dark and drear,
must   While my dear lad maun†face his faes
slopes   Far, far frae me and Logan braes.†

2

Again the merry month of May
Has made our hills and vallies gay;
The birds rejoice in leafy bowers,
The bees hum round the breathing flowers;

[180]

Blythe Morning lifts his rosy eye,
And Evening's tears are tears o' joy:
My soul delightless a' surveys,
While Willie's far frae Logan braes.

3

Within yon milk-white hawthorn bush,
Amang her nestlings sits the thrush:
Her faithfu' mate will share her toil,
Or wi' his song her cares beguile.
But I wi' my sweet nurslings here,
Nae mate to help, nae mate to cheer,
Pass widow'd nights and joyless days,
While Willie's far frae Logan braes.

4

O, wae upon you, Men o' State,
That brethren rouse in deadly hate!
As ye make monie a fond heart mourn,
Sae may it on your heads return!
Ye mindna† 'mid your cruel joys   remember
The widow's tears, the orphan's cries;   not
But soon may peace bring happy days,
And Willie hame to Logan braes!

O, WERT THOU IN THE
CAULD BLAST

1

O, wert thou in the cauld blast
  On yonder lea, on yonder lea,
My plaidie†to the angry airt,†   plaid;
  I'd shelter thee, I'd shelter thee.   quarter
Or did Misfortune's bitter storms
  Around thee blaw, around thee blaw,
Thy bield†should be my bosom,   shelter
  To share it a', to share it a'.

2

Or were I in the wildest waste,
  Sae black and bare, sae black and bare,
The desert were a Paradise,
  If thou wert there, if thou wert there.
Or were I monarch of the globe,
  Wi' thee to reign, wi' thee to reign,
The brightest jewel in my crown
  Wad be my queen, wad be my queen.

YESTREEN[†] I HAD A PINT O' WINE

Last night

1

Yestreen I had a pint o' wine,
  A place where body saw[†]na;
nobody saw
Yestreen lay on this breast o' mine
  The gowden locks of Anna.

2

The hungry Jew in wilderness
  Rejoicing o'er his manna
honey
Was naething to my hiney[†]bliss
  Upon the lips of Anna.

3

Ye monarchs take the East and West
  Frae Indus to Savannah:
Give
Gie[†]me within my straining grasp
  The melting form of Anna!

4

There I'll despise Imperial charms,
  An Empress or Sultana,
While dying raptures in her arms
  I give and take wi' Anna!

5

Awa, thou flaunting God of Day!
  Awa, thou pale Diana!
Each; go
Ilk[†]Star, gae[†]hide thy twinkling ray,
  When I'm to meet my Anna!

6

Come, in thy raven plumage, Night
  (Sun, Moon, and Stars, withdrawn a'),
And bring an Angel-pen to write
  My transports with my Anna!

POSTSCRIPT

1

The Kirk an' State may join, and tell
  To do sic[†]things I maunna:[†]
such;
 mustn't
The Kirk an' State may gae to Hell,
  And I'll gae to my Anna.

2

She is the sunshine o' my e'e,
  To live but[†]her I canna:
without
Had I on earth but wishes three,
  The first should be my Anna.

MEG O' THE MILL

1

O, ken ye what Meg o' the mill has gotten?
An' ken ye what Meg o' the mill has gotten?
She's gotten a coof†wi' a claut o' siller,† dolt; hoard
And broken the heart o' the barley miller!   of money

2

The miller was strappin, the miller was ruddy,
A heart like a lord, and a hue like a lady.
The laird was a widdifu',† bleerit knurl†– gallows-
She's left the guid fellow, and taen the churl! worthy;
                 dwarf

3

The miller, he hecht†her a heart leal and loving. offered
The laird did address her wi' matter more
  moving:
A fine pacing-horse wi' a clear,† chainèd bridle, bright
A whip by her side, and a bonie side saddle!

4

O, wae†on the siller – it is sae prevailing!† woe; potent
And wae on the love that is fixed on a mailen!† farm
A tocher's†nae word in a true lover's parl,† dowry; speech
But gie me my love and a fig for the warl!† world

FINIS

INDEX OF FIRST LINES

(including choruses)

INDEX OF TITLES

Since many of the poems are known by their first lines, titles not listed below may be found in the *Index of First Lines* beginning on page 185.